CW01335029

*Travels in*
*Radical Christianity*

ROY PEACHEY

# Travels *in* Radical Christianity

Angelico Press

First published in the USA
by Angelico Press 2024
© Roy Peachey 2024

All rights reserved

No part of this book may be reproduced or transmitted,
in any form or by any means, without permission

For information, address:
Angelico Press
169 Monitor St.
Brooklyn, NY 11222
angelicopress.com
info@angelicopress.com

ISBN 979-8-89280-037-2 pb
ISBN 979-8-89280-038-9 cloth
ISBN 979-8-89280-039-6 ebook

Cover design: Michael Schrauzer

For my family and all
those who helped me on the way

# Acknowledgments

I am extremely grateful to the many people who welcomed me into their homes and communities while I was writing this book. I am in awe of the faith, hope, and love I have seen in so many people's lives. Since so many people have helped me, it would be invidious to mention individual names, but I can assure you all that I am deeply grateful.

As always, John Riess and his team at Angelico Press have been most helpful (and patient). My family has also been amazingly tolerant. Time and time again, I have tentatively suggested another trip. Time and time again, they have allowed me to go off on my travels with good grace. I dedicate this book to them and to all who have helped me along the way.

# CONTENTS

1 Victor Beamish  1

2 The Bruderhof  6

3 The Franciscans of the Renewal  22

4 The Manquehue Apostolic Movement  35

5 Opus Dei  48

6 The Catholic Worker Movement  62

7 The Transalpine Redemptorists  77

8 Home Education  91

9 L'Arche  108

10 Margaret and Barry Mizen  118

11 Radical Orthodoxy  130

12 Back to the Parish  143

# 1

# Victor Beamish

ON March 28, 1942, an experienced pilot called Victor Beamish climbed into his Spitfire for the last time. Aged thirty-eight, he was in command of RAF Kenley, an important airbase just south of London, and so was no longer required to fly sorties himself. However, with the Second World War still raging, he was determined to lead from the front. Having been invalided out of the air force with tuberculosis in 1933 before making a spectacular comeback in 1937, he was never going to be content with a desk job while his men were flying missions to combat the Luftwaffe threat. Victor Beamish was a hero, a veteran of the Battle of Britain, one of Churchill's "few" to whom so much was owed by so many, but on that spring day in 1942 he ran into trouble over Calais. Giving chase to a group of Messerschmitts and Focke-Wulfs, he himself came under fire and crashed into the English Channel. His body was never found.

Victor Beamish may not be a household name but he is not entirely forgotten in Kenley. A quiet street that leads to the now empty aerodrome has been named for him: an inconsequential road for a man of great consequence. It is a tribute of sorts, but a curious one. There are no houses along Victor Beamish Avenue and scarcely any cars. It is a sleepy side street that leads to a public space that is used primarily by dog walkers and families with young children. It is a place we visit when we want somewhere safe for our children to ride their bikes. A place where terriers and spaniels greatly outnumber cars.

At the end of Victor Beamish Avenue, Kenley Aerodrome exists in that middle space which appears after work stops and before heritage begins; neither booming nor abandoned, it hosts gliders at weekends and model planes controlled by excited children or, more often, by their excitable fathers. It seems hard to believe that this was once a vitally important base in two world wars, an airfield that King George VI visited, a place on Hitler's hit list. Every once in a while there is a flurry of activity: a couple of replica planes are wheeled in and '40s swing music is played through temporary speakers but, for the most part, Kenley Aerodrome is quiet, slightly dilapidated, and empty. One or two buildings still remain from its glory days but most of these are deserted too. There is no museum, no historical reconstruction, and no obvious attempt to use the site to revive the local economy.

At least there was no sign of rejuvenation until the moment some workmen started to clear the site of the old NAAFI building. Weeds were grubbed up, parts of the building were rebuilt, and a couple of football pitches appeared. Then a sign appeared on the front gate, announcing that the building was now the Kenley Campus of Focus School. Intrigued, I made further enquiries and discovered that the derelict building had been bought by the Plymouth Brethren Christian Church. When I mentioned the church to my mother-in-law, a doughty and often unconventional woman, she didn't seem at all surprised, launching into a story about how, in her younger years, she and my father-in-law, both good Catholics, had allowed the Brethren to use a room in their house for their Sunday gatherings. This continued until a body was brought into the house for a funeral, an event which drew the church to the attention of the local council, which quietly moved it on. I pressed my wife for further details but all she remembered was hiding upstairs when "the Christians" arrived in their smart suits and not daring to re-emerge until the hymn-singing stopped. She didn't know whether the brethren she remembered as a child were connected with the group which had set up a school in Victor Beamish Avenue or not.

Perhaps it was this knowledge gap that made me keen to learn more. Or perhaps it was the striking absence of people on the site whenever we cycled past. Where were the teachers? Where were the children? Where were the open days, school fetes, and community events? The Plymouth Brethren seemed to keep to themselves to an extraordinary degree. After a little research, I discovered that members of the Plymouth Brethren Christian Church attempted to live lives that were both in the world and radically separated from it. None of their members attend university, which means that they have to recruit teachers from outside the church. However, those teachers have to work within very clear parameters, not doing anything to challenge the group's strict Biblical literalism. The children themselves are also kept away from potentially damaging influences. That is why we never saw them walking home at the end of the school day. Of course, this approach to education raises all sorts of questions. What access do the children have to the internet, the radio, or any other sources of information about the wider world? How are they prepared for adult life? What career options are open to them if university is not on the cards? What view of the world do they develop in such an enclosed community? I decided that there was only one way to find out: I would try to arrange a visit.

**Searching for roots**
In retrospect, I realize that emailing was probably a mistake. If you want to find out more about a technology-averse community, knocking on the front door is probably a better introductory stratagem. Nonetheless, I emailed and waited for an answer. As I waited, I kept my eyes and ears open: I didn't find out anything more about the Plymouth Brethren Christian Church but I did stumble across more and more groups that espoused one form or another of radical Christianity.

These groups came from different religious traditions and often had quite different approaches to discipleship, but they also shared a fundamental orientation towards the cultures in which they found themselves. In each case, they had made a conscious decision to separate themselves to some extent from that surrounding culture, living a life rooted in a distinctive, counter-cultural understanding of the world. That is what makes them radical: their roots—which is what the Latin word *radix* means—are planted in a different kind of soil. Or maybe in the same soil but with a different fertilizer. Or possibly even in the same soil but in a different bed. I wasn't sure and I wanted to find out.

Radical Christians were everywhere, it seemed: the Bruderhof;

*Travels in Radical Christianity*

the Franciscan Friars and Sisters of the Renewal; L'Arche; the Transalpine Redemptorists; Opus Dei; Manquehue; the Catholic Worker Movement. I couldn't even escape their radical pull in my academic studies. Having started a PhD with Tracey Rowland, whose *Culture and the Thomist Tradition* was published by Routledge's Radical Orthodoxy imprint, I transferred to the University of Nottingham to study with Alison Milbank and found myself at the epicenter of Radical Orthodoxy.

The reason I found all these intentional Christians—to use the current jargon—so interesting was that my own ideas had been developing in what might be considered a radical direction. This was something of a surprise to me because I thought I had given up any vestiges of radicalism in my early twenties. Having grown up in a broadly conservative environment, I shocked my parents by announcing that I was going to work for a night shelter after graduation. Making a basic tactical error, I let slip just how little I would be earning and unwittingly sent them into the sort of tailspin Victor Beamish had spent his career avoiding. They weren't happy but the decision had been made, so off I went to the intriguingly named St George's Crypt in Leeds to work with hundreds of down-and-outs. Situated conveniently next to the Leeds General Infirmary—a place I ended up checking into much more often than I would have hoped to—the Crypt, as it was known locally, was a basic shelter and day center that had been set up by a crusading Anglican clergyman in the 1930s. I stayed there for just over a year before moving on to historical research in Cambridge, having had my incipient youthful radicalism beaten out of me.

The low point came when I self-pityingly dragged myself to the local doctor's surgery the day after being attacked by a drunken down-and-out while I was trying to prevent him from entering the shelter in his extremely inebriated state. It took a couple of us to control him as he lashed out, and I thought we had just about got the situation under control when he headbutted me. When I woke up the next day, my nose was still throbbing with pain, so I took myself off to the doctor's to find out if it had been broken. My GP was not terribly sympathetic. "Is it usually that shape?" she asked, before telling me that, even if it was broken, there wasn't a lot that could be done about it, which meant that I left the surgery with insult added to injury, with a nose complex and an aching head. Suddenly an obscure PhD in early-seventeenth-century history seemed like an extremely attractive option. I sent in my application and looked forward to three violence-free years.

Without ever consciously thinking about it, I soon slipped into the belief that radicalism is little more than an aspect of youthful exuberance that we should discard as soon as we develop enough wisdom and practical experience of the world to settle down. I went to Cambridge, abandoned the PhD, got a job as a schoolteacher, and started on my journey towards comfortable, middle-class respectability. However, years later and to my great surprise, I found that I could not shake off a number of radical ideas. I became interested in home education (which is definitely a radical option in the UK) and then in unschooling (which is off the scale). I also became a Catholic, which placed me outside the mainstream, and found that the deeper I immersed myself in the Faith the more I became attracted to ideas that were deemed radical in contemporary British society. The lure of radical Christianity was slowly swinging round my head.

It was unsettling to find that the philosophies by which I had lived my life now seemed deficient in some way. This uncertainty shook my political convictions, but I soon became convinced that political labels did not get to the heart of the radical Christianity that I was learning about. To describe radical Christians as left- or right-wing, conservative or progressive—surely one of the most misleading and unhelpful words in current political discourse—does not get us close to understanding what they are all about. I became convinced that I had to move beyond politics if I was to get to grips with the essence of the groups I was stumbling across. Instead of labeling them, I wanted to get to know them. Instead of standing at a distance, I had to find out more. That meant I had to go on a journey with no real sense of where that journey might lead. Without waiting any longer for the Plymouth Brethren Christian Church to reply, I set out on my travels.

# 2

# The Bruderhof

DOVER IS A PLACE most people leave in a hurry. Europe's busiest ferry port, it hosts over two million cars, even more trucks, and close to one hundred thousand coaches each year. Most of the twelve million or so passengers passing through each year are keen to get someplace else, which is a pity, not just because Dover's ailing economy could do with their money, but also because Dover itself has some incredible treasures, most notably the famous white cliffs and the impressive Norman castle that perches on top of them.

The surrounding countryside is equally fine. The rolling Kentish hills are home to a fabulous array of birdlife, including sandwich tern, grey plover, and house martin (which may be the original blue bird that soared over the white cliffs of Dover), as well as some equally impressive plant life, such as rock sea lavender, early spider orchid, and viper's-bugloss. Even the place names are intriguing: Frogham, Ratling, Pett Bottom, Shatterling, and Ripple can all be found a few miles from the port.

And then there's Nonington, a tiny village a couple of miles off the A2, the main road that leads from Dover to London: a place that tourists and truck drivers bypass without even knowing it is there; the place I was determined to find that spring morning. Nonington used to be chiefly known for its College of Physical Education, which was set up in 1938 by the English Gymnastic Society and closed in 1986 when demand for PE teachers slumped. For ten years the site lay derelict until the Bruderhof bought it and set up their Beech Grove community.

The Bruderhof, meaning "place of brothers," was founded in 1920 by a German Lutheran couple, Erberhard and Emmy Arnold, along

## The Bruderhof

with Emmy's sister, Else. The three of them had become concerned about the gap between the life actually lived by Christians and the radical lifestyle the Gospel seemed to demand. Searching for another way to live their faith, the Arnolds set up a community in central Germany and, inspired by the writings and example of the early Anabaptists, adopted the name Bruderhof.

With the rise of Hitler in 1933, the community, which advocated non-violence, was forced to leave the country. They settled first in England, where their numbers grew considerably, and then in Paraguay when the English interned Germans during World War II. Struggling with an unfamiliar environment and with the problems that war brought, the Bruderhof barely survived the next few years, but slowly expanded into the USA and back into Europe in the years after the war. In 1999 they established a community in Australia and, three years later, returned to Germany. Today there are twenty-four communities on four continents, though the total number of members is still small: something in the order of three thousand people.

The Bruderhof approach has evolved in the last hundred years and, like many other communities, it has had its problems. The community had a major upheaval at the start of the 1960s but, since then, has re-established itself as a peaceful, outward-looking, intentional group. Alone among the many communitarian groups that emerged in Germany after World War I, it has not only survived until the present day but, crucially, has also retained its radically Christian stance.

Many similar groups have either stayed Christian while becoming gradually less radical or have remained radical while shedding their Christianity, the Quakers offering a telling example of both tendencies. I used to live close to Swarthmoor Hall in the English Lake District, where George Fox, the founder of the Quakers, lived. In his day the Quakers were extremely radical, which is why they were persecuted, but the religion has now evolved into an organization that George Fox would struggle to recognize. Contemporary Quakers may or may not be politically and religiously radical and may or may not be Christian. When I visited Swarthmoor Hall a few years ago, for example, I was met by the director of the center, who told me that he was a Buddhist Quaker.

The situation with the Bruderhof seemed rather different, so I was eager to find out more about the reality of their community today. I was especially intrigued because I had only come across Anabaptists in books. When studying the Protestant Reformation in high school, we concentrated on Luther and Calvin, making only a short diversion into the Anabaptist experiment at Münster, where a Dutch tailor called Jon of Leiden led a revolutionary kingdom in which, as one recent museum exhibition put it, "rebaptism was made compulsory, goods were held in common, polygamy was legalized, and there was an orgy of iconoclastic destruction." Such a threat to the status quo provoked an immediate response in the tempestuous sixteenth century, the city coming under siege and being quickly captured. After a brief struggle, Jon of Leiden and other Anabaptist leaders were executed, their corpses being displayed in iron cages hung from the steeple of one of the city's churches as a warning to others. As one historian wrote, Münster had quickly become "a byword for religious and political anarchy [and its specter] haunted mainstream Protestants and provided Catholics with a convenient stick with which to beat their confessional enemies for more than a century."

A few years later—about the time I started and then quickly abandoned my PhD on early-seventeenth-century Protestantism—I came across Q, a bold, rollicking, 672-page novel about the events in Münster, though I have to confess that the only reason I bought it was that the four anonymous authors chose Luther Blissett as their *nom de plume*. Blissett was a great soccer player who played for Watford and England before, improbably, joining A.C. Milan at a time when most Englishmen ventured onto the European continent only for cheap booze. I found the combination of footballing legend and radical Protestantism irresistible and so bought the novel immediately, without waiting for it to appear in cheaper paperback form.

All of which is a long-winded way of saying that I didn't know a great deal about Anabaptists that spring morning and the little I knew did not sound very encouraging.

### Counter-cultural education

There is a fundamental difficulty when writing about any counter-cultural group. It is easy to write about what the group *doesn't* do. This sense of difference may be intriguing—it may even be what makes the group attractive—but focusing on difference can be profoundly misleading. The first problem is that such an approach is essentially negative. Rather than picking up on the positive achievements of the community, we describe its strangeness. Rather than trying to understand, we stand outside and judge. The second problem is that it encourages us to focus on external issues, which can lead us away from the core motivation of the group, the reasons for their radical choices.

How the Bruderhof differentiated themselves from the surrounding culture was obvious before I reached their main entrance. As I drove down a narrow country lane, slightly unsure of where to find the community, I spotted two women walking down a side road. They were wearing head scarves and long, unfashionable dresses. I knew instantly that I had reached my destination: no one else dressed like that in Kent. I turned into the road and parked my car, from which moment other differences soon became apparent, the most significant being that I appeared to have entered a technology-free zone. As I was given a tour round the site, which consisted of a central meeting hall, a factory, a school, and lots of houses, I was struck by the absence of cars and screens. In a world dominated by technology, the Bruderhof stood out by turning their back on TVs, mobile phones, and computers. The difference from the world I had just left was very clear: what I couldn't tell was just how deep-rooted that difference might be. I thought I could perhaps determine that while a couple of tenth-grade students gave me a tour of the school.

Coming from the high school where I taught at the time, which was overladen with technology, I was really struck by the absence of Smartboards, TV screens, and laptops in the Bruderhof school. Even more striking was the use of chalk and blackboards (or, to be more accurate, greenboards): the school clearly eschewed the use of electronic media on principle. In other ways the school seemed perfectly straightforward, though the uniform was certainly unusual. The girls all wore the long dresses and *Kopftuchen* (head scarves) I had noticed on the way in, and the boys, whose haircuts were distinctive for not being distinctive, wore slacks and simple, logo-free shirts.

*Travels in Radical Christianity*

The American curriculum was certainly unusual for a school in the UK, but the Earth Science lesson I dropped in on was fascinating, as was the mix of students, a boy with Downs Syndrome working happily with his classmates. There was certainly nothing to worry any educational inspector, though they might well have been surprised by the handwriting lessons and the politeness of the students.

Nonetheless, as I continued with my tour, I did come across occasional reminders of the world I had just left: a computer room (albeit an empty one); the headmaster discreetly taking a call on the only cell phone I saw all day; and the microphone that was used to introduce the midday community meeting. Above all else, there was the factory.

**A Bruderhof business**
A highly successful business venture, this factory, which manufactures play equipment for young children, is built on some rather surprising foundations, the most obvious of which is that no one in the business is paid. In fact, no one in the Bruderhof community is paid for his or her work. The headmaster, the farmer, the factory worker: each is paid the same amount, which is nothing at all. The lack of remuneration certainly didn't stop the Bruderhof from working: at one end of the factory was an area where the elderly could continue to work for as long as they chose to do so. Suitable tasks and suitable seating were provided so that everyone could do their bit for the business. Bruderhof workers do not retire until they choose to.

In fact, the production line was so finely honed that any member of the community could slip into place, pull down the instructions for a particular job, and get to work. However, to my surprise, given what I had seen elsewhere, this communitarian approach was underpinned by the latest technology. The business thrives because of the strong design principles that are applied to its products, and those designs are created electronically as well as on paper. On the same site are homes that have broken free from the technological snare that has been set by the modern world and a factory that harnesses the very best aspects of technological modernity.

For critics of radical Christian groups like the Bruderhof, this split is clear evidence of a fundamental contradiction at the heart of radical Christianity: while overtly rejecting the modern world, these backward-looking romantics are, in reality, making use of its benefits. You can't publicly turn your back on Facebook, Netflix, and Amazon at home, as the Bruderhof do, while exploiting technological resources at work. It's worse than inconsistent: it's smug and hypocritical. So the argument goes.

### Anabaptist technology

But the argument is misguided. The Bruderhof are not mindless naysayers. Their attitude to technology is not hopelessly inconsistent. In a fascinating article on "Anabaptist Technology" in their highly professional magazine, *The Plough*, John Rhodes, the director of development for a Bruderhof business, sets out four principles. The first is that families and community come first. Human relationships always take precedence over technology, especially any form of technology that pushes us in the direction of passivity rather than creativity. That means that technology is restricted to the working day: "We seek to push back against the pressure, enabled by technology, to allow daytime work to spill over into times that should be reserved for our families or for the community."

The second principle is that technologies have an agenda. Picking up on the work of Neil Postman and others, he argues that technology is never neutral. In fact, "many technologies are designed to turn us into consumers." These first two principles lead to the third, which is that screens and children don't mix. That is why pupils practice handwriting in Bruderhof schools. That is why their children don't have cell phones. That is why the Bruderhof community I visited was a remarkably quiet and peaceful place. Summing up the Bruderhof approach to education, Rhodes writes that "the heart of education is not the transfer of knowledge, but the nurturing of relationships" and that "academic learning, while important, takes second place to the more central educational task of growing in relationships, and in fact often occurs as a side benefit to it." One of the strengths of the Bruderhof approach to life is that it is not just grounded in a clear belief system but resists the lure of ideological rigidity precisely because it is built around people.

And the fourth principle? "Don't be afraid to walk away." This may be the simplest of the four principles but, in some ways, it is the toughest. How many of us are truly able to ditch our phones, our TVs, our email accounts? We like to hang on to what we have, even when we are uneasy about its impact on our lives. The problem with the electronic media, as writers from Marshall McLuhan to Neil Postman, Albert Borgman, Matthew Crawford, Nicholas Carr, and Sherry Turkle have convincingly shown, is not so much the content it purveys as the behavior it encourages. Because we are human we get tired—we are not disembodied minds floating free of material existence—and because we get tired our resistance drops, which means that we vegetate in front of the TV or flit between websites or scroll through increasingly meaningless "content" on our phones. Because we are human, we can very easily neglect what makes us most human, which is relationships. That is why Bruderhof members leave their laptops in the workplace. That is why they don't use social media in the home. That is why there isn't a TV to be seen in their communities. Rather than focus on technology, they focus on people. Without people, and without the hard work of building relationships with people, there is no community, and building community lies at the heart of the Bruderhof project.

**A commitment to the real**
You can't build community without running up against reality. There is nothing theoretical about the Bruderhof project. In fact, what all the communities in this book share is a commitment to the real; they reject Cartesian dualism and insist on some form of embodied education instead. The Bruderhof keep electronic media from their children not because they are nostalgic Luddites nor because they believe in some mythical Golden Age. They keep electronic technology from their children because they want them to celebrate reality instead. In their view, both celebration and joy spring from an engagement with real people, tangible objects, and the created world. This is what matters to them: not closing their eyes to the benefits of technology. The idea that radical Christianity stems from a rejection of the world is about as far from the truth as you can get. It is precisely because they embrace the world that the

# The Bruderhof

Bruderhof work so hard to create a viable community. Focusing on the obvious external differences between their lives and the majority of ours can obscure this simple but decisive fact. The Bruderhof project is essentially a practical one: how to create a sustainable community in a world that is increasingly individualized and atomized. Community building is the root of their radicalism.

I was able to experience this community to a limited extent after my tour of the school when I was invited to the midday community meeting. I had no idea quite what would be involved. A silent prayer meeting on the Quaker model? An extended Bible Study? A business meeting complete with agenda and minutes? What I found in the central hall was about two hundred chairs arranged in concentric circles. Though one man led proceedings through an incongruous microphone, there was clearly a determination to steer clear of anything that smacked of hierarchy in the community. The meeting began with us all being taught a new hymn, which was not as surprising as the fact that the hymn was in German. A new family from Germany had joined the community and were sharing their talents and knowledge with the others. After the German hymn, we launched into a series of hymns in English, all with an Easter theme. I found this decision disconcerting because we had only recently entered Lent, but, as my guide later explained, though the Bruderhof broadly follow the liturgical calendar, they are not constrained by it. The Bruderhof work happily and creatively with many Catholics, including Cardinal Dolan in New York and the Franciscan Friars of the Renewal. They publish the work of Dorothy Day, Gerard Manley Hopkins, and Óscar Romero. They regularly quote St Augustine and St Teresa of Calcutta, but they retain a Protestant suspicion of what they regard as external show. You won't find religious images and statues in their communities; fasting and abstinence is not part of their practice; simplicity is valued and ritual is not. The Bruderhof do not have churches or chapels: the people are the church and buildings are seen as impediments to a lively relationship with God. The spirit of Early Modern radical Protestantism, albeit purged of its knee-jerk anti-Catholicism, lives on in their communities.

To a Catholic convert from evangelicalism who has grown to love the richness of the liturgy and the liturgical year, this simplicity was attractive but incomplete. There are certainly many occasions when I yearn for more silence in the liturgy, for more reverence in church, for singing that comes close to being in tune, but what sustains me at those times is the knowledge that silence, reverence, and beautiful music are all central parts of the Church's tradition, even though they are honored as often in the breach as in the observance. Though I was greatly impressed by what I found in the Bruderhof community, it seemed to me that these good people still lacked something hugely important.

**Foundations**

Despite my reservations, I was profoundly moved by what I experienced in Nonington, mainly that the whole community came together with such obvious common purpose and joy. The source of this joy is clearly a lively faith in God, but the form it takes owes a great deal to a decision the Arnolds made after they founded their community in 1920. Looking for inspiration and guidance, they turned to the early Anabaptists and saw in them much of what they were seeking for the twentieth century. The Anabaptists rejected any notion of a state church and focused instead on creating an intentional community, which is why adult baptism mattered so much to them. At least one group of Anabaptists—the Hutterites—also believed that they should renounce private property and hold all goods in common. It was this radical decision that brought the wrath of the authorities of the day down upon them and it is this aspect of the Bruderhof philosophy that is most striking today.

The Bruderhof also drew inspiration from other people, among them the educational reformer Friedrich Froebel, who created the concept of kindergarten. That is why "Bruderhof schools seek to provide each child with a happy and constructive childhood and to educate the whole child," as their foundational document puts it; "this includes rigorous academic instruction; craftsmanship and practical skills; singing and the arts; unstructured play and sportsmanship; and the experience of nature." The importance and role of children in the communities is striking. In the meeting I attended, the hymns were chosen by a different person each time, someone calling out a number and the whole community launching into the hymn. Sometimes it was an adult who chose but, just as often, it was a young child. In an age where children are often marginalized, sexualized, or exploited by marketing that is hell-bent on getting them to become grown-up consumers, this respect for children and childhood is rare. There was no accompaniment when we sang, but that meant the whole community, children and adults alike, could be heard creating a unified hymn of praise.

**Reclaiming conversation**

Having experienced the midday community meeting, I confidently expected that we would all eat together, but the midday meal, though prepared in the communal kitchens, took place in family homes. It was a privilege to be invited into a family's home, so I will not abuse their trust by laying out what was private for all to see. All I will say is that the homes, like the rest of the community, are run according to exactly the same principles of unadorned, technology-spare simplicity. Which meant that we had time to talk.

Sherry Turkle has lamented the dying art of conversation in her book *Reclaiming Conversation: The Power of Talk in a Digital Age*. Seventy years ago, George Orwell did much the same, remarking that "in very many English homes the radio is literally never turned off, though it is manipulated from time to time so as to make sure that only light music will come out of it. I know people who will keep the radio playing all through a meal and at the same time continue talking just loudly enough for the voices and the music to cancel out. This is done with a definite purpose. The music prevents the conversation from becoming serious or even coherent." Many of us may agree with Turkle and Orwell about the desirability of good conversation and the impediments that technology places in its way, but few of us are able, like the Bruderhof, to take the next step and actually do something about it.

Over lunch, I asked my hosts why Bruderhof communities are usually situated in rural locations. The answer was not that the community wanted to flee from a world it no longer trusted, but rather that these rural settings allow them to have a deeper experience of reality. In a world that is becoming virtual, they wanted to have an existence that was grounded in the physical. There is certainly no sense that the Bruderhof have cut themselves off from the world. Community members help Syrian refugees in Jordan, provide disaster relief throughout the world, run programs in schools aimed at breaking the cycle of crime, and help run soup kitchens. They also host many guests each year in their international communities, many of whom come from quite different religious and social backgrounds. This shocked a school inspector who found Rowan Williams, former Anglican Archbishop of Canterbury and Master of Magdalene College, Cambridge, teaching a class at one of the Bruderhof schools shortly after she asked the headmaster whether his pupils were exposed to other points of view.

Nonetheless, it is easy to see Nonington as something of a rural idyll. The Bruderhof drive their horses and carts at local shows; their cows supply organic dairy products for the community; their buildings are often beautifully designed. Was it possible, I wondered, to maintain a community like this in towns and cities? Was the rural setting essential to the enterprise? A few weeks later I had the chance to find out when I was invited to the small Bruderhof community in south London.

**A community in the city**

There is a tension at play in the work of the Bruderhof. They value their rootedness, being in one place long enough to become part of the wider local community, but their fundamental commitment is to the community as a whole, which means that they have to be ready to go to whichever Bruderhof community needs them at a moment's notice, wherever it might be. Because they aim to be self-sufficient, their doctors, teachers and architects have to be prepared to travel across the world to where they are needed most. That was why I was invited to London to meet a member who was flying in from New York.

One of the most remarkable Bruderhof projects is *The Plough*, a wonderful magazine that draws on an incredible range of writers, from Rowan Williams to Roger Scruton, from Dorothy Day to Óscar Romero. Wanting to find out more, I was invited to meet one of the editors when he flew into London for the London Book Fair and so experienced a typically Bruderhof paradox: rather than rely

## The Bruderhof

on Skype or other technology, the editor wanted to meet potential writers in person, but to do so, he had to rely on intercontinental air travel and the advanced technology that goes into making such flights possible.

Not that I had the opportunity to ask him about aircraft technology: we were meeting to discuss Slow Education, an offshoot of the Slow Food movement that was bringing together an Anabaptist like him and a Catholic like me. But first I had to find the Bruderhof's London site. Stepping out of the Underground station, I found myself in a slightly rundown, and entirely anonymous, part of London. Eventually I found the right street and wandered past several rows of terraced houses and a lot of overflowing dustbins. On the corner of the street stood the Golden Anchor pub—a dingy, run-down building—a few dilapidated shops and a scrap metal dealer, outside which were heaped old sinks and radiator parts. Next door to the scrap metal dealer was the grandly named Fantasy Tattoo Parlor, which had an intriguing notice in the window: "No Children. No Alcohol. No Drugs. No Dogs." It seemed a strange combination. Just beyond the tattoo parlor was the even more grandiose Emmanuel Miracle Temple Bethany Fellowship of Great Britain (Minister, Rev. Dr Prince J. Blackson D.D.) It wasn't as run-down as the shops or the pub, but it didn't appear to be thriving either.

Among all this anonymity, grandiosity, and seediness, the Bruderhof community stood out. A brightly colored cart, some well-tended flowers, and a sign reading "Free Books Here" stood outside one of the otherwise anonymous houses. Never one to knowingly sidestep a free book, I worked my way along the bookcases in what appeared to be a converted garage, finding books in Spanish and German and English, conversion stories, tales of reconciliation, back issues of *The Plough*, and *The Gospel According to Gerard Manley Hopkins*. There was also a friendly notice telling browsers that they could pop in for a chat if they wanted to. I took a few books and rang the bell.

The Bruderhof's London community was small, so small in fact that there was only one person home when I visited. The other members were either visiting their families in one of the other communities or studying at one of London's many universities, for the

Bruderhof don't share the Plymouth Brethren Christian Church's aversion to higher education. However, since they are fully aware of the dangers and temptations that cluster round universities and colleges, they ensure that their young adults have a safe base to return to while studying. This time I wasn't offered a guided tour, because there was so little to see, but that simply emphasized the importance of people over buildings in the Bruderhof communities. There are no Bruderhof churches for a reason: places gain significance from the people who live in them as far as the Bruderhof are concerned. Community building may be easier to achieve away from the distractions and difficulties of the city, but communities can be built wherever people are. The presence of the Bruderhof in rural Kent and rural Sussex is as much a practical response to the world as an ideological one: since their communities are self-sustaining there is no need for them to be built in central conurbations where property is expensive and space is limited. From the outside, the Bruderhof's radical lifestyle looks like a carefully considered rejection of an increasingly secularized world: from the inside it looked more like an eminently practical reaction to the realities of the day.

**Back to the countryside**
Having visited two of the Bruderhof's three English communities, I still had questions, so that summer I paid a visit to Darvell, the largest of the three. Having visited Beech Grove, I found Darvell less of a shock. It too had a large campus with a small factory and a school. It too was home to a wide range of people of different nationalities, backgrounds, and physical conditions. The oldest person I met was a 106-year-old who had just returned to the community after years away. One of the most attractive aspects of Bruderhof communities is their wholehearted inclusiveness: the elderly and infirm are an absolutely integral part of the community. In fact, the only difference between Darvell and the community at Nonington, as far as I could see, was that Darvell was bigger. I had landed at headquarters.

I arrived just in time for the midday communal meal, which began with a rousing song and ended with a few notices. Again I was very warmly welcomed but again I was struck by the absence of

## The Bruderhof

religion in the place: we didn't say grace; the song wasn't a hymn; and, with the exception of some plain wooden crosses worn by the woman, there was little sign of any religious iconography. What matters to the Bruderhof is social behavior. It is not enough to read the story of the rich young man; you have to live in poverty yourself. It is not enough to call for peace, you have to live in peace with all and refuse to "serve in the armed forces of any country, not even as noncombatants." It is not enough to talk about the importance of community, it has to be lived. The Anabaptist way, as revived by the Bruderhof, is quintessentially practical.

Living that kind of radical Christianity is tough, so I probed deeper to learn how the community has survived for a hundred years without sacrificing its radical principles, as so many other Christian groups have. However, the members to whom I spoke seemed strangely uninterested in the question. For them, it was simple: they were Bible-believing Christians and they stuck to the Word of God. "We are not a joining community," one of them told me. "We have to be called." What this meant in practice was that "vocations" were strongly put to the test before any final commitment was made. Mission has always been important to the Bruderhof, but they value deep-seated commitment over a mere increase in numbers.

This testing approach can be seen in a fascinating book, *I Put Away My Sword: An Iraqi Soldier's Journey from Battlefield to Brotherhood*, written by a member of the Darvell community, Yacoub Yousif. Yousif trained as a chemical engineer at Baghdad University before being called up into the Iraqi army at the time of the Iran-Iraq war. The horrors of this time rekindled his dormant Christian faith and also provoked in him a loathing of war. After many traumas, which are vividly set out in his book, Yousif and his wife, Layla, managed to escape Iraq for Sweden, where they first learned about the Bruderhof. When they first approached the community with a view to joining one of the English settlements, it was suggested that they set up their own community in Sweden rather than join the one at Darvell. This they dutifully did before later moving to England, only for the community to advise them to return to Sweden to work on their relationship and consider their calling. It was another six years before they returned to Darvell and became full members.

I met plenty of interesting and friendly people during that visit to Darvell, though I rarely had a chance to ask whether they were lawyers, doctors, or some other profession by training. None of this mattered to the Bruderhof: they were simply brothers and sisters. It was only when I visited Darvell, for example, that I discovered that one of my guides around the Nonington community had a PhD: he was certainly never referred to as Dr Kim. What the members had in common was more important to them than their professional differences, which is one reason they maintained a uniformity of dress. Not that this uniformity and lack of adornment (including a striking absence of makeup for women) led to a sense of drab uniformity: what I noticed instead was the essential differences between people: differences of personality, in particular. What mattered was not how fashionable you were or how physically attractive you were, but how you responded to others.

**Catholic questions**

My visits to the Bruderhof communities were fascinating, but what I really wanted to know was how far the Bruderhof model could be replicated in other settings. In fact, what I wanted to know above all else was whether such a response to the modern world was desirable or possible for Catholics. That was another reason I was interested in Yacoub Yousif's story, for he had grown up as a Catholic and had, for a while, contemplated becoming a priest. In the end, he did not find what he was searching for in the Catholic Church, and I found that unbearably sad. It would be tempting to take issue with some of the theological judgments he expressed in his book, but to do so would be largely to miss the point. If Yousif had found the loving community he sought within the Church, he would, almost certainly, have had his theological doubts resolved. Instead, he, who had been brought up in the Catholic Church, now lived in an Anabaptist community. Would that, I wondered, have been the case if Catholics had set up similar communities? And, if they did, what would an authentically Catholic community look like? How would it differ from the Bruderhof model? Had anyone actually created

## The Bruderhof

one that worked? To answer those questions I needed to continue my travels. Having visited Darvell, I had to move on. Or rather move back. My next port of call would be the 1998 Winter Olympics.

# 3

# The Franciscans of the Renewal

IN 1998, the Winter Olympics were held in Nagano, Japan, and a young American speedskater called Kirstin Holum was keen to make her mark. She was young and had big skates to fill because her mum (who also happened to be her coach) had been the youngest person to compete in the world championships before going on to become a world sprint champion and Olympic gold medalist.

Kirstin had been the junior world champion herself, but she was now competing at senior level and that was a very different proposition. Her first race was the 3000 meters, and she surprised many people by placing sixth; and in the next event, the 5000 meters, she placed seventh: a pretty impressive achievement for a seventeen-year-old. With the Olympics over for another four years, Kirstin considered her future. Rather than continue with the punishing schedule required if she was to perform at the very highest level, and with some doubts whether Olympic success could ever bring true and lasting happiness, she decided to go to art school instead, where she focused on photography (if you'll forgive the pun).

Kirstin had first felt called to the religious life during a pilgrimage to Fatima the year before the Olympics, but that call, though powerful enough at the time, had now been all but forgotten. She was a Catholic who recognized the limitations of the Olympic ideal, but she was not prepared for the spiritual darkness that would confront her at art school: lacking Christian friends, she began to drift away from the strong Catholic faith in which she had been raised. She still attended Mass on Sundays, but the lively faith in which she had grown up and the powerful call she had received at Fatima became distant memories.

After graduation, she returned home to live with her mum, who was active in her parish and in pro-life work, which is how Kristin ended up praying outside an abortion clinic when a group of vibrant young Catholics who were on a pro-life walk across America passed by. Never having seen young Catholics so on fire with their faith before, she was deeply shaken. So much so that the next day, to her mum's great surprise, she announced that she was going with them. And so her pilgrimage began, a pilgrimage that ended (in one sense) a short while later when the group arrived in Toronto for World Youth Day, but that continued long after that momentous month (in another sense) because Kristin met another powerful group of witnesses in Toronto: the Franciscan Sisters of the Renewal. Having first heard the call to religious life in Fatima as a sixteen-year-old, Kristin rediscovered her vocation. After a period of discernment, she realized that she truly was called to be a bride of Christ. Taking the name Catherine, she served in the Bronx and then moved to the Franciscan convent of St Joseph in Leeds, in the north of England.

### Renewing the tradition

The Franciscan Sisters of the Renewal were founded in 1988, shortly after a group of Franciscan Friars, including Fr Benedict Groeschel and Fr Andrew Apostoli, came together to form a new community in response to what they saw as a crisis in religious life. Dismayed by the death rattle of Catholic religious life in the English-speaking world and northern Europe, they were even more dismayed that it was "not dying a holy death. Despite the presence of large numbers of older religious men and women who often yearn for the spirituality and obedience that they knew when they entered the life, some religious communities are filled with dissent from official Church teaching and even the norms of Sacred Scripture."

Fr Benedict and the other friars were clear-eyed about the causes of the crisis they saw all around them, but much more important than that analysis were their individual responses to it. Fr Benedict wrote movingly about his moment of truth in *A Drama of Reform*:

*Travels in Radical Christianity*

One evening, an earnest young Capuchin priest warned me that vocations were being lost. "We must do something," he said. I heard a voice answer him, "Yes, we will do something." The voice was my own, but I had made no act of the will to say these words. I was so shocked by what I had said that I almost jumped up. Despite its troubles, I loved the community to which I belonged, and of course I still love the Capuchin ideal. A cold shudder ran through my body. I went to the chapel to pray. I felt both anxiety and relief. That visit to Christ in the Blessed Sacrament convinced me that I had a serious moral obligation to try to do something effective. I did not even think to raise the question, *Do others have a similar obligation?* I was only deeply aware of my own obligation. If I did not do something, I knew I would commit a mortal sin of negligence and omission, a lasting and habitual sin that could be forgiven only when I had fulfilled the obligation to try.

What this obligation meant in practice was starting a new community and stripping away everything but the essentials from the friars' lives. Fr Glenn Sudano, one of the other founding friars, explains what that meant in very material terms: "Most days," he wrote, describing the work they did in their first friary in the Bronx, "were spent scraping, stripping, pulling up, and tearing up—we call it Capuchinizing—getting rid of the old, ugly, unnecessary things such as paneling, rugs, and wallpaper. The rectory parlor became our chapel almost as soon as the tabernacle replaced the television. All the old air-conditioning units were put outside, to the delight of local drug addicts." It also meant returning to a life of total poverty, as they had promised in their vows. The Bruderhof may be counter-cultural in living without any form of income, but the Franciscan Friars of the Renewal take this counter-cultural radicalism to a whole new level. They are not paid, but neither do they run their own profit-making businesses. Their mission is to live with and for the poor, which means that their friaries are situated in places of great social and material deprivation, from the Bronx to Comayagua, Honduras, to the East End of London and Bradford in the UK. It also means that they exist on the mercy of God and rely wholly on the generosity of others. At their founding, Fr Benedict

# The Franciscans of the Renewal

went to see Mother Teresa, who was staying in New York, and explained that they only had eight hundred dollars and eight men. "Don't worry," Mother Teresa told him, "God has lots of money." She was right.

However, the success of the Franciscan Friars of the Renewal is not down simply to a romantic renunciation of money. Mother Teresa gave them another gift when she encouraged them to have a Eucharistic holy hour as part of their daily community schedule. The Franciscans are busy people, running soup kitchens, leading retreats, caring for the downtrodden, and doing pro-life work, but they also pray for five, six, or seven hours a day. Having stripped away the inessentials, they made sure they held firm to the essentials. Each month the friars spend a day or two in silent prayer away from the noisy cities where they live and work, and each Friday they usually spend the day in prayerful silence. As Fr Benedict Groeschel explained:

> Although the brothers and sisters lived in the inner city, surrounded by violence and all of the problems that New York knew at that time, our formation stressed silence and prayer. You can be silent and prayerful on the subway if you make up your mind to do so. We never felt the need to move to a quiet country setting and start a formation program in some beautiful valley. Our formation houses were poor, plain, and simple.

## Surprised by joy

I didn't know about the weekly schedule of prayer when I invited Sr Catherine to visit our school on a Friday. She still came and, what's more, she brought another sister with her. She and Sr Chiara—who didn't stop smiling with joy at the fact that she had recently made her profession—spent a couple of days with us and made an immediate impact. "Those nuns are so happy!" one of my students told me in obvious bemusement. My student's bemused response got right to the core of the sisters' vocations: they may have been Franciscan Sisters rather than (cloistered) nuns, but they were certainly happy. In fact, more joyful people you could not possibly hope to meet. It is tempting for the English to put this down to cultural differences, but there was much more to their joy than a lack of

English reserve: they were clearly sustained by some inner resource that we seemed to lack, so I was as fascinated as my students by what Sr Catherine had to tell us.

Speaking to a group of students and local parishioners that evening, she talked about the Olympics and showed us her USA team jacket. She spoke about World Youth Day, which her mum had earlier tried to persuade her to attend without success, and the impact it had on her when she had eventually found herself there with the young pro-life pilgrims. She told us about the importance of the witness of young Catholics and encouraged us in our own journeys; but in a sense it wasn't what she said that mattered, but the witness she gave by her life and by the way she spoke, with such assurance of the love of God. When it came to the Q and A session, most of the obvious questions we had prepared seemed utterly irrelevant. We didn't need to ask her about what she missed because she was so clearly brimful of happiness with the life she had chosen. There was no need to ask about boyfriends or children because we could see what it meant to her to be a bride of Christ. And we didn't need to ask her about ice skating, because we could see that she was more fulfilled in religious life than she could ever have been with Olympic success. Nonetheless, we couldn't resist asking whether she had ever been on the ice since becoming a sister. Just once, she said, but as she was whizzing round—while still wearing her habit—one of the attendants beckoned her over and told her to slow down.

"I wasn't even going that fast!" she said with a broad smile.

Listening again to Sr Catherine's testimony, I was struck by her emphasis on the importance of prayer and confession. Talking about the pro-life walk across America, she stressed how important fellowship with other young Catholics had been, but she also spoke about how being on pilgrimage had given her exactly what she needed: time away from the usual pressures and commitments; time to give herself to God in the company of other Christians; and regular reception of the sacraments.

When Sr Catherine returned to our school a year later with some other sisters, I heard similar stories, albeit without the Olympic flavoring. Sister Faustina Joseph of Jesus Through Mary is an English sister who obtained a PhD in biochemistry before taking her religious vows. Like Sr Catherine, she had found her college years spiritually difficult. What changed her was not a long walk but an extended period of immobility after a serious car accident. Forced to take stock of her life—and with the time to do so—Sr Faustina realized that she had become more concerned with what her friends thought of her than with living the life God wanted for her. In religious life, she found the life she had been seeking for so many years without consciously realizing what it was—or rather Who it was—she sought.

Sr Faustina may have been looking in the wrong places for fulfilment before she became a Franciscan sister, but she was not entirely lost: in seeking the approval of her friends, she was acting on a dim realization that she could not exist as an isolated individual. The people around us matter and the way we interact with others matters. Whether we realize it or not, we are all part of some kind of community, however inchoate or dysfunctional that community might be; in taking her vows of poverty, chastity, and obedience, Sr Faustina was committing herself to another type of community, one that was centered not on the fulfilment of its members' needs but on the service of the poor. It was also clear that, in serving others with others, she found more fulfilment than she ever had done by trying to please her friends.

### Franciscans in the city

Intrigued by these sisters and especially by the extraordinary joy they exuded, I decided to track down the Franciscan Friars of the Renewal to see if I could get to the root of their way of life, to see if they shared the same fruits of the Spirit. I also wanted to find out what sort of community they had established. Was it essentially the same as the Bruderhof communities or was there something fundamentally different? I wasn't sure if a trip to the East End of London counted as a pilgrimage, but I figured that it was time to set off on my travels again, "following the Lord with headlights but without a road map," as the Franciscans themselves put it.

I may not have had a road map but I did have a guide in a person whom I shall call Mary, an exceedingly jolly lady who lived nearby, one of whose relatives is a Franciscan Friar of the Renewal. Mary volunteered each week at the friars' soup kitchen in the East End of London, so she kindly offered to give me a lift and to introduce me to the friars. En route, she regaled me with stories about Youth 2000, an international Catholic movement for young people which had been important in her own journey of faith, about converting to Catholicism from Anglicanism, and about her relative. "I only prayed for him to become a Christian," she said with a beaming smile, "and then he became a friar!" Mary is wonderfully enthusiastic about the Faith and is also quintessentially English, frequently breaking off mid-tale to say, "Oh, Roy, it was such a hoot!" But this enthusiasm was no substitute for practical action: when we arrived in Canning Town, she opened the trunk of her car and pulled out bags of food and drink for the friars and for the homeless people they serve.

St Fidelis Friary in London is an unprepossessing building which reminded me of an old-fashioned scout hut. Besides the friars' quarters, there is a kitchen and eating area where the homeless are welcomed twice a week for lunch and once a week for a change of clothes. Having been invited to a soup kitchen, I had visions of trestle tables being set up outside and generous helpings of soup being ladled out of enormous vats for local down-and-outs. The reality was a sit-down meal that was brought to the homeless at their tables. "It's like a restaurant," one of the friars explained to a new guest. "We'll serve you at the table."

It really was like a restaurant. Nando's had donated lots of chicken, which was served with a wonderful rice dish, a delicious-looking sauce, and plenty of bread. For those who still had room for more, there was plenty of watermelon too. As Mary introduced me to all and sundry as "Roy, who's writing a book," I decided to take a back seat and get on with the washing up. Writing a book suddenly seemed like an indulgence when there were people to serve and the work of God to be done. Stepping back also enabled me to listen to the ebb and flow of conversation. If we live in an age when the art of conversation has been lost, the message clearly hadn't got through to this part of Canning Town. Not that the friars were voluble: quite the opposite in fact. They were friendly, welcoming, and noticeably less bubbly than the sisters I had met, but they shared with the sisters a determination to be present to and for others. This, rather than the grey robes and bushy beards, is what truly distinguishes them from so much of society.

Without external distractions, like phones and TVs, and with a living faith built on the real presence of Christ in the Eucharist, the friars are free to concentrate on what really matters: other people and the work of God. That is why there was no sense of anxious rush that day, in marked contrast with most working environments I have experienced. The friars were unhurried and the homeless men and women were given the time they needed to eat, chat, or keep to themselves. I tried to put my finger on what else was different from the year I had spent working in a night shelter in Leeds. The profile of the homeless guests was certainly not what I had remembered. In the 1990s, the majority of the homeless men I met were Irish or Scottish. Now they were mostly central or eastern Europeans. But the differences lay deeper than that. What was most striking was the lack of tension in the building. My memories of working in a night shelter cluster around fights, threats, and barely suppressed violence. By the end of my time in Leeds, I came to dread each evening shift, not because I was hit that often but because the threat of violence was always there. The Friars of the Renewal are not immune to the same pressures, but the atmosphere was certainly much calmer. One of my main tasks at the night shelter was gate duty, a euphemism for a task none of us wanted: smelling the breath of homeless men to see if they had been drinking, sniffing glue, or taking harder drugs. If they had, we were supposed to turn them away. If we did, they tended to turn on us. The main duties in St Fidelis Friary, by contrast, seemed to be preparing and serving a meal. It was much more civilized.

Working in a night shelter, I was almost always on edge, but the friars seemed remarkably laid-back. When I worked in Leeds I never felt fully in control: the friars, by contrast, know that God is in control, which means they are much more relaxed than I ever was, and not just when dealing with the local homeless population. As the conversation turned to a Youth 2000 festival in Walsingham that Mary was trying to persuade me to attend, one of the brothers cut through the uncertainty by simply suggesting that I ask God whether He wanted me to go and then to let Mary know. His response to a question about a particular book was similarly relaxed: "I don't know," he said; "I only have a Bible and a copy of the Catechism." Mary wasn't convinced. "Don't take any notice of that," she said. "He went to Steubenville." Indeed he had. His education at the Franciscan University of Steubenville had prepared him for life as a friar in ways that most universities scarcely touch. In a word, he had learned discernment. Some things matter: others don't. Some things matter at certain times but not at other times. Books can be taken up, but they can also be set aside.

Sadly, my own powers of discernment are less well honed. I now had a clearer sense of the Franciscan way of life but wasn't yet sure what it meant for me. And not just for me. The Franciscan Friars and the Franciscan Sisters were tremendously impressive, but I wanted to know what the laity, especially those of us who are married, could learn from them. There seemed only one way to find out: I would have to go to Walsingham. Or rather, we would have to go. This was a task for the whole family. Some lines from *The Lord of the Rings* came to mind as I tried to work out what to say to my wife:

> The Road goes ever on and on,
> Down from the door where it began.
> Now far ahead the Road has gone,
> And I must follow, if I can,
> Pursuing it with eager feet,
> Until it joins some larger way
> Where many paths and errands meet.
> And whither then? I cannot say.

Before I left the friary, I spent a few minutes in the chapel. Like the rest of the building, it was very simple, even austere. A few wooden chairs, the altar and tabernacle, the San Damiano crucifix before which St Francis prayed at the beginning of his ministry, and a picture of Our Lady of Guadalupe. As Fr Benedict Groeschel once explained, "This austerity of imagery is intended to direct our attention, and our devotion, to Christ, especially in the mystery of his Sacred Heart and the Divine Mercy." It was a good way to begin a pilgrimage.

# The Franciscans of the Renewal

**A pilgrimage to Walsingham**

After a long drive and several traffic jams, we drew close to Walsingham. It was a stormy day in late August and we were nervous about putting up our tent, but, as we drove along Norfolk's sempiternal roads, a double rainbow appeared in front of us. We drove on, heartened.

The storm broke shortly after our arrival. After a quick meal in the communal food tent, we realized that we had little choice but to get on with pitching the tent, since our youngest child was exhausted, and sleeping in the car was not a viable option. Reluctantly stepping out into the elements, we tried to wrestle the tent into submission, which eventually we managed, though only after breaking one of the tent poles in the process, which left us with a rather lopsided sleeping place. We were too tired and wet to greatly care.

Pilgrimages are often completed in trying circumstances. I look back with great happiness on significant trips to Rome, Lourdes, and Altötting, the great Marian shrine near the birthplace of Pope Benedict XVI, and remember not just moments of spiritual growth but also times of great difficulty. The two go together. From the Holy Family's journey to Bethlehem to their pilgrimage to Jerusalem twelve years later and right through to the revelation granted to the disciples on the road to Emmaus, the Gospels are full of examples of suffering being turned to the good as the people of God left their homes and set out on the path that God had set before them. I cannot claim that the difficulties we faced at the start of our pilgrimage to Walsingham were anything more than a temporary inconvenience, but there was a sense that we had put ourselves out and so, in taking ourselves away from our comfortable quotidian existence, we had laid ourselves open to whatever it was that we had been brought here to learn.

One of the first pilgrims we bumped into was Sr Catherine Holum: she was smiling as usual. She updated us on Sr Chiara's return to the USA, chatted about Youth 2000 and the work of the Franciscan Friars, and then, as is the way at festivals, the crowds swirled another way and we were off to the next event. Youth 2000

*Travels in Radical Christianity*

was founded by a young Englishman called Ernest Williams in response to John Paul II's call for young people to witness to Christ as the new millennium approached. Recognizing the spiritual poverty that afflicts so many people in our materially rich world, Williams realized the urgent need for young people to discover or rediscover the riches of the Faith: the Holy Mass, Adoration of the Blessed Sacrament, the Sacred Scriptures, the Sacrament of Reconciliation, Devotion to Mary, the Mother of God, and the fullness of the Church's teaching. Finding an annual home at the ancient pilgrimage site of Walsingham, therefore, seemed entirely appropriate.

Walsingham is a curious Marian shrine. Its importance in English religious history is undoubted, but its early history is obscure. According to the Pynson Ballad, written in the late fifteenth century, the shrine was established in 1061 when Our Lady led Richeldis de Faverches in spirit to Nazareth and asked her to build a replica of the house where the Annunciation took place. However, we don't have a great deal more information than that and very few sources from the first centuries of the shrine's existence. Whatever the exact origins of the shrine, it is clear that it soon became one of the most important pilgrimage sites in Europe. Many English kings visited the shrine, including Henry III, Edward I (who visited on many occasions and believed that Our Lady of Walsingham had saved him when a ceiling collapsed in the room where he was playing chess), Richard II, Henry V, Henry VI, Edward IV, Henry VII, and, most surprisingly of all, Henry VIII. In 1511 he visited Walsingham to give thanks for the birth of a son—who died several weeks later, thereby changing the course of English history—and made regular payments to the shrine for years after that until, abruptly, he embraced Protestantism and turned against Walsingham and every other pilgrimage site in the country. The shrine to which he had paid so much devotion became the victim of his iconoclastic fury.

Henry VIII's wanton destruction of the shrine meant that when the sanctuary of Our Lady of Walsingham was restored in 1897 it was placed not in Walsingham itself but in nearby King's Lynn (which had itself been called Bishop's Lynn before Henry VIII got his hands on it). However, the previous year a Catholic called Charlotte Pearson Boyd had bought the fourteenth-century Slipper

## The Franciscans of the Renewal

Chapel just outside Walsingham and restored it to Catholic use. This tiny place was the last of the wayside chapels on the way to Walsingham. It was here that pilgrims—including Henry VIII in his day—removed their shoes so they could complete the last mile of the pilgrimage barefoot. It is here that the Catholic National Shrine of Our Lady is based and here too that Youth 2000 used to meet each year. What this all means in practice is that it is entirely possible to go on pilgrimage to Walsingham without ever making it to Walsingham itself; a pilgrimage to the Catholic National Shrine of Our Lady is always a reminder that we are on our way to a final destination that we have not yet reached. Pilgrims traveling to Walsingham find themselves at the center of life while knowing that they are also on the margins.

It seemed apt, therefore, that the final talk we attended at Youth 2000 was given by one of the Franciscan friars on St Juan Diego and Our Lady of Guadalupe. Like many of the saints to whom Our Lady has appeared, St Juan Diego lived at the margins of society. He was neither rich nor powerful, which is perhaps why no one believed him when he first spoke about the apparition he had seen. His story is strikingly similar in that sense to St Bernadette's in Lourdes, though there are differences too, not least what happened when St Juan Diego's bishop asked for a sign as proof that the Lady really was who she said she was. Returning to the bishop with his tilma—his cloak—full of roses that had inexplicably bloomed in mid-winter on top of Tepeyac Hill, Juan Diego tipped them onto the floor as proof. Even more amazing was the sight that greeted them when they looked at the tilma in which the roses had been carried, for imprinted there was a glorious image of Our Lady. Standing in front of the sun with her foot on the crescent moon, she wore a blue-green mantle decked with the stars in the exact position they appeared in the night sky on December 12, 1531, the last day she appeared to Juan Diego. With her eyes looking downwards in prayerful devotion and her hands joined in prayer pointing to a cross at her neck, she wore a black band to indicate her pregnancy. This was the image of the Mother of God miraculously given to Juan Diego. This was the image the Franciscan Friars of the Renewal had come to talk about.

*Travels in Radical Christianity*

Standing in front of a consecrated copy of the original, two friars recounted the story of St Juan Diego, explained the symbolism of the holy image, and told us how the tilma, which is made of cactus fibers, has survived almost five hundred years without any sign of deterioration, despite the fact that this material usually disintegrates within a few decades and despite the fact that it was subjected to an acid spill in 1791 and a dynamite attack in 1921. The story of the image of Our Lady of Guadalupe is extremely inspiring, but both the story and the image point to a greater truth: what changed Juan Diego's life and the lives of thousands, if not millions, of people in subsequent years was an encounter. An encounter with Our Lady, who always leads us to Christ. It is this ongoing encounter with Our Lady that gives the Franciscan Friars and Sisters of the Renewal their raison d'être. It is in their encounter with Our Lady that they find their joy and their vocation. Their undoubted radicalism is a byproduct of this essential meeting: not a means in itself or even a consciously chosen position. The encounter comes first: everything else follows from it. Having grasped that basic fact, we were able to leave Walsingham, knowing that we had found the source of radical joy and peace we had been seeking, even if that encounter—and that joy and peace—still had to be sought and experienced anew daily.

Our time with the Franciscan Sisters and Friars of the Renewal was inspiring, but meeting them turned out not to be the end of my journey. Stepping out of the tent where we had learned so much about St Juan Diego and Our Lady of Guadalupe, we were about to head back to our car when we bumped into some friends. They were chatting to a group of Chilean Christians who had come to Walsingham from Chile via Downside Abbey, so we joined them for a few minutes. What we heard then opened our eyes to another form of radical Christianity. It didn't take us long to realize that our travels were about to take another direction.

# 4

# The Manquehue Apostolic Movement

I HAD VERY LITTLE EXPERIENCE of Catholicism as a child. An excellent but rather fearsome French teacher was a Catholic—which somehow added to his mystique—as were our next-door neighbors, an Irish construction worker and his extremely jolly wife, though what their faith meant to them in practice was entirely mysterious to me. All I knew was that, while my brothers and I wandered downhill to the local Church of England primary school, their children slogged uphill to the local Catholic school.

Catholic ideas also passed me by at school until I started studying the Reformation at the age of sixteen, at which point I quickly decided that I was on the side of Martin Luther against the corrupt Catholics, with their funny ideas about purgatory, indulgences, and prayers to Mary. A.G. Dickens, one of the Protestant historians whose work we read, would have been proud of me. By the time I left school, I was, therefore, afflicted by an unwholesome combination of ignorance and prejudice. It was only when I continued my historical studies at university that a few doubts snuck in.

Studying the sixteenth century, I continued to focus on the Protestants—men like John Foxe, whose *Book of Martyrs* was a wildly over-the-top account of the wickedness of "Bloody Mary" and the heroic virtues of the Protestant martyrs who resisted her evil rule—rather than on their Catholic opponents. However, I also attended a series of lectures by Christopher Haigh, a revisionist historian who enjoyed upending the reputations of the historians who had preceded him. Historians like A.G. Dickens, for example, whose work he memorably described as John Foxe with footnotes. Comments like these shook my unthinking, old-fashioned Protestantism but they didn't quite set me on the path to the Catholic Church. I still knew what I was against even if I wasn't quite so sure what I was for, which meant that I was in danger of becoming an intellectual cynic. With mind and heart divided, I threw myself into the certainties of evangelical Anglicanism, attending very long services (where I made notes on very long sermons), going on university missions to Bedford and Salisbury, and joining every prayer breakfast and lunchtime meeting I could find.

I pushed the claims of the Catholic Church away, but my interests were catholic in one sense at least. Having spent the summer before I went up to university reading lots of novels, the first thing I did on arriving at university was ask if I could transfer from History to an English degree. The answer was no. Taking the decision on the chin, I decided that I wouldn't let a degree get in the way of my genuine interests, so I spent as much time reading literature, theology, and psychology as I did working my way through the very long historical reading lists we were given each week. As a consequence, I tumbled across some really important ideas that got under my skin and put down roots, to mix my metaphors. Confusing the college librarian, who expressed great surprise when she discovered I was actually studying history, I borrowed books on topics as diverse as Robin Hood, Sylvia Plath, Freudianism, and what I was supposed to be studying, the Anglo-Saxons, and adopted the same approach to lectures, attending a series on memory, a series on the Vikings, and a series on St John's Gospel given by a Dominican at Blackfriar's. It may have been there that I first came across Simon Tugwell O.P.'s two wonderful books on prayer, which made a huge impression on me, though even then I skipped over the more obviously Catholic references. I lapped up what he wrote about the Desert Fathers but skated over the section on liturgical prayer, largely, I suspect, because I had no experiential understanding of what he was writing about.

And so it continued over the three years of my degree. My Christian formation was provided by evangelical Anglicans, with Catholics occasionally suggesting that there might be an alternative path.

## The Manquehue Apostolic Movement

I took a course on International Calvinism, for example, only to discover that my tutor, a wonderful Scottish woman called Jenny Wormald, was a Catholic. I became a huge C.S. Lewis fan and, through him, discovered the work of Catholics such as G.K. Chesterton and J.R.R. Tolkien. I even ended up reading St Augustine's *Confessions* in Latin when I signed up for the course on Christians and pagans in the late Roman empire, though I thought of Augustine as a proto-Protestant rather than as a Catholic saint. I still have the books I bought the summer I graduated: they make a curious collection that gives some indication of my interests at the time: Michael Polanyi's *Meaning*, Alistair McGrath's *Reformation Thought*, Trevor Huddleston's *Naught for Your Comfort*, and Tolkien's *Tree and Leaf*.

By that stage, I was keen to escape Oxford's rarefied atmosphere and so I applied to an evangelical charity that placed young people in challenging social settings, which is how I ended up at a night shelter in Leeds. Being roughed up in Leeds provoked little more than a desire to return to the rarefied atmosphere of university life, which is why I moved back down south. Having a vague idea that I wanted to study popular Protestant devotion and an even vaguer idea that the Meyer-Briggs scale would enable me to unlock the topic, I applied for a PhD in early-seventeenth-century history at Cambridge and was offered a place. My initial supervisor was Patrick Collinson, an eminent biographer of Archbishop Grindal, one of Queen Elizabeth's faithful divines, but I was soon transferred to another supervisor, about whom I knew next to nothing. His name was Eamon Duffy and he was about to publish *The Stripping of the Altars*, a book that transformed the way historians look at the pre-Reformation Church in England. I sometimes look back and wonder how my life might have been different had I stuck with the doctorate, but I had already decided that studying for a PhD was a mistake and so I pulled out. I had been in Cambridge for only twenty days.

Over the next ten years, I drifted between Anglican churches, sometimes turning up on Sundays and sometimes not. Having also drifted into teaching, I completed a stint in a school on the edge of the English Lake District and then got a job at the London Oratory School, where I met lots of Catholics, though I still paid little attention to the claims of the Church itself. Moving on from the Oratory School after a couple of years, I ended up in another school that also happened to be Catholic and continued my churchless existence. However, the divine angler was beginning to reel me in. I was now engaged to one of the Catholics I had met in London and so found myself driving up to Yorkshire one day to meet some monks she knew there. By this time, I was more clued up about the Catholic Church than I had been during my undergraduate years, but I had certainly never met a monk before and found the whole concept of giving up one's life to live in a monastery completely baffling.

It was a long drive up to Yorkshire but eventually we arrived at our destination, having driven through some of the most beautiful countryside in England. Ampleforth Abbey is partially sheltered in a valley on the very edge of the Yorkshire moors, but it is still very much exposed to the elements. As you look down from the abbey and the school, the landscape sweeps away over rugby and cricket pitches to a distant wood and beyond into the Vale of York. Turn the other way, and the land rises steadily until you reach a plateau of gorse, bracken, and sphagnum moss. Sometimes the moors can still be covered by snow in April. But what I remember chiefly about that visit was not the weather but the wonderful food—Benedictine hospitality really is very good—and a fascinating conversation with one of the monks as we strode out over the Yorkshire moors together. He didn't convert me immediately, but he dealt with each of my objections to the Church with strong arguments and good humor, which set me off on a path that would lead to surreptitious instruction from a priest in a nearby parish and my reception into the Church a few months before the fiancée who had taken me to Ampleforth and I were married.

### Discovering *lectio divina*

After that initial experience in a Benedictine monastery, I was happy to return most years for the Easter Triduum. Hotfooting it from school at the end of term, we arrived on Holy Thursday, so that we could relive the slow agony of Good Friday, experience the long wait of Holy Saturday, and then attend the glorious Easter Vigil in the abbey church. Now that I was in the Church, the hang-ups that had held me back for so long slipped away. Now that I was inside, I grew to love the liturgy and was quickly bowled over by the Benedictine tradition. The liturgy lay at the heart of the Easter retreat but, in between services, there was also a program of talks, some of which also made a big impression on me. It was in one of these talks that I was introduced to *lectio divina*.

Unusually, the monk who was giving the talk—the same monk who had listened to me chuntering away about my objections to Catholicism as we strode across the moor some years before—was joined by some laymen. They were members of the Manquehue movement from Chile, who had been living at Ampleforth for a couple of years, helping to create *lectio* groups with the students. I had vaguely heard of Manquehue from one of the mums at my daughter's school, but the more I heard during those few days in Ampleforth the more impressed and intrigued I became. At the heart of the movement was a fundamental commitment to *lectio divina*. *Lectio* was something of a mystery to me, but the Chileans I met gave me an introductory leaflet which explained that it is simply:

- A special way of reading the Word of God contained in the Scriptures.
- Reading with faith that God is speaking to me here and now.
- Reading with great attention, slowly, meditatively, savoring each word.
- A way of reading so active that it engages the whole person.
- A way of reading where one surrenders, allowing oneself to be seized by the Word of God.
- An intimate contact with Jesus Christ, our Lord and our brother, who is present in Sacred Scripture.
- To listen to the Lord in his Word and to respond to Him in loving prayer.

**A lay Benedictine community**

The Manquehue Apostolic Movement, to give its full name, was founded in 1977 by José Manuel Eguiguren Guzman, but the story of its founding goes back several more years to a time of intense spiritual desolation that José Manuel had experienced. Politically, it was a dark time in Chile and José Manuel was struggling to make sense of his life, concluding at one point in his early twenties that "there was no sense in life; one was born, lived, worked and died and it meant nothing," as Patrick Barry has written in his book about the movement, *A Cloister in the World*. Into this darkness strode a Benedictine monk, Fr Gabriel Guarda from the Holy Trinity Monastery in Las Condas. He invited José Manuel to the monastery for a chat and listened as the young man poured out his troubles. What surprised José Manuel was Fr Gabriel's response: rather than give answers of his own, he suggested that they pray to the Holy Spirit and turn to Scripture. And so it continued for each of their meetings: Fr Gabriel listened to the confused young man and then suggested Bible passages that they could read together. The listening didn't stop when they opened the Bible: in fact, it intensified. The key to José Manuel's healing was that he learned, in the presence of a wise Benedictine monk, to listen to God in the Scriptures, to discover the Word in the word, and not to treat the words of the Bible as objects to be analyzed and put to one side.

These meetings continued almost daily for three years. Three years! How often do we look for quick answers in our hasty world? José Manuel needed answers but he was prepared to wait. Or rather, he was prepared to take his time to explore and to listen really deeply. One writer, drawing on the work of St Irenaeus of Lyon, has written of the haste of sin and the slowness of salvation. That description seems to match José Manuel's experience exactly. It took him three years to emerge from his period of spiritual confusion, at which point he was ready to transform the lives of those around him. Dropping into his old school, the Manquehue School in Santiago, he offered his services to the headmaster, expecting to be given some history teaching. Instead the headmaster asked him to take the Confirmation class. The idea horrified him, but he accepted the request as a call from God and then tried to work out what to do. The obvious approach, he concluded, was to speak to the eighteen-year-olds—who were being confirmed largely for social reasons—about his own experiences, to listen to them, and to share his own experience of the transforming impact of *lectio divina*.

By the end of the process, it had become clear to José Manuel and to eight members of the group that what they had started together could not end there, and so, after consulting with Fr Gabriel and meeting with Cardinal Raúl Silva Henriquez, they tentatively founded the Manquehue Movement, unsure about the direction it should take but certain that the "basic characteristic of this Movement can be summed up in one word—friendship—Christian friendship—Christian love."

The development of the movement, like the development of José Manuel's own relationship with God, was slow and sometimes unsteady, but it continued to grow, rooted in the Benedictine life José Manuel had learned in the Holy Trinity Monastery. The group was uncertain about the future, but they believed that they were being called to form a cloister in the world and that what this meant in practice would become clearer as they prayed, lived, and worked together in a stable, faithful community. They began on a small scale, setting up *lectio* groups in a local parish and working with the poor in local settlements called *campamentos*. As the movement grew, separate communities were established for men and women, but José Manuel was concerned about the long-term development of the movement, since it was entirely dependent on the goodwill of parish priests who could themselves be moved on. He also keenly felt the lack of a formal educational venue and started to think about founding a school. With support from his family, José Manuel started to plan, finding a suitable building on the lowest slopes of the Manquehue mountain in Santiago and staying in close touch with Fr Gabriel, who realized that, if the school was to be truly Benedictine, advice would have to be sought elsewhere. The person he turned to was Fr Dominic Milroy, who was Headmaster of Ampleforth School in the UK and whose mother was Chilean. When José Manuel wrote to him for advice, Fr Dominic suggested that the only way he could really understand Benedictine education was to visit a Benedictine school in person. He invited José Manuel to Ampleforth.

Certain themes of radical Christianity kept recurring during my travels. One is the importance of community; another is the importance of travel itself. In my own search, I had to leave my daily existence behind, if only temporarily, to discover other ways of living the Gospel. More importantly, the radical Christians I was encountering had also made their own journeys, their own pilgrimages of faith. With a school that had no pupils, José Manuel set off on a journey from Chile to northern England to see what he could learn about Benedictine education. What impressed him most about Ampleforth was the life and work of the monastery itself. He also made some important personal contacts that were to help sustain the new movement. Some of the monks were very helpful, but one of the most significant meetings was with a student who showed him round the school, Nicholas Duffield—the first of many English students to make the reverse journey from Ampleforth to Chile to work as a *gringo* with the Manquehue movement.

After a second visit to Ampleforth in 1982, José Manuel managed to open his new school, San Benito, beginning a new stage in the work of the Manquehue movement: "Here was a venture," Fr Dominic Milroy explained, "that was entirely lay, entirely from scratch, entirely unsupported and unfunded by existing clerical institutions and at the same time entirely rooted in the Rule of St Benedict and the concrete traditions of Benedictine education." What makes the Manquehue movement distinctive—what makes it radical—is this development of the Benedictine tradition. As Fr Patrick Barry points out, this "was not simply a matter of borrowing a few spiritual principles of monasticism and applying them to lay life." José Manuel and his colleagues created a truly Chilean, truly lay, truly Benedictine spirituality that has continued to transform lives to this day.

**From *acogida* to *tutoría***
One way of understanding this Chilean form of Benedictine spirituality is to look at certain key words or concepts, the first of which is *acogida*, a Spanish word for "welcome." That at least is its basic meaning, though *acogida* "is stronger than the English word and in the movement from an early stage it became a key word to express not only welcome but also the generous affirmation of and commitment to another person in charity." Another important concept for the burgeoning movement was *convivencia*, a word that means "living together." *Convivencia* was used by the Manquehue especially to describe a monthly meeting for *lectio divina* over a meal. These

meetings, needless to say, were not business meetings but an opportunity to demonstrate *acogida*. Another key word is *tutoría*, which has a rather different connotations from the English "tutor" or "tutorial." For the Manquehue movement, the *tutorías* are opportunities for older students to get together with younger students in groups for *lectio divina*. They are the primary means by which older students are able to form the faith of younger students and provide a wonderful example of how the apparently intractable problem of peer pressure among teenagers can be resolved.

These elements of Manquehue spirituality were not simply plucked out of the air but were drawn from the centuries-old Benedictine tradition. At the heart of the Manquehue movement, in other words, is the Rule of St Benedict applied to the modern world. This decision to put the Rule at the center of all their work was an absolutely crucial one. As the movement grew—as the core community took vows of chastity and were joined by married Oblates—a clear structuring principle was required. At first, there was some uncertainty about what to do with the Rule but it quickly became apparent that it had to be placed at the center of their community's life: "they began to take it very seriously indeed and to consult it for practical guidance in their everyday life and work." Adopting the Rule of St Benedict, they really were able to create a cloister in the world, seeing "their monastic commitment as fidelity to the teaching of St Benedict with these principal differences—that it includes married Oblates and their families and that the cloister in which they live is determined not by the physical encirclement of walls but by the defined locations of their prayer together and their work together in the world." Placing the Rule of St Benedict at the center of their community, they were able to consolidate and sustain the new movement. Placing the Rule at the center, they were able to step out into the world with a clear vision and purpose, as José Manuel explained:

> Jesus told his disciples: "a man can have no greater love than to lay down his life for his friends." In order to live this love we need community. Chapter 72 of the Rule is clear about this and it is our constant point of reference. This love cannot be theoretical

love. It must be real and personal. I am convinced that our parents commend their sons and daughters to us because they love them. Our schools must be a place where we can prolong that family love. In carrying out this task *tutoría* is irreplaceable. It is the guarantee of that personalized love. In this light I have no doubt that *tutoría* is the soul of each of the Manquehue schools.

## Renewing the tradition again

Over time, the movement continued to grow, taking on two more schools and opening a retreat house in Patagonia, at the southern tip of Chile. However, growth was not itself the aim. Rather than open yet more schools and establish a sort of Benedictine franchise, José Manuel took the bold decision to send members of the community abroad. In fact, he sent them to Britain where, at the request of various Benedictine abbeys, they began the work of reinvigorating the ancient tradition on which they had themselves drawn.

The problems facing the English Benedictine communities have been well documented in recent years. Many deep-rooted issues have now been brought into the light and the future for some communities is far from certain. However, even before the recent crisis, it was clear that the Benedictine tradition in the UK was under pressure. When I first visited Ampleforth, there were a good number of young monks and a small but steady stream of vocations, but then some of the monks left and the vocations began to slow down. A similar story could be told of many other Benedictine communities. At Worth, the age profile of the monks is steadily increasing. The community at Farnborough is so small that it had to let the National Catholic Library go. The Benedictine school at Belmont has closed because of a lack of numbers. Even Buckfast Abbey, which seemed to be undergoing something of a revival, has issues of its own.

Into this picture of decline, Chilean laymen from the Manquehue movement have added a new layer of color, or, to adapt the metaphor, they have not only started to restore the original painting but have also begun to transform it. Another way of thinking of their work is to imagine not a gallery of slightly faded Old Masters but Westminster Cathedral, the English mother church. One of the most wonderful aspects of this glorious piece of Byzantine architecture tucked away in the center of London is the fact that it isn't yet finished. Building work was begun in 1895 and was finished eight years later, but the internal decoration has continued sporadically over the years as the funds have come in. Side chapel by side chapel, mosaics have appeared, adding light and color to the cathedral's grand expanse, the glorious blues and golds of the magnificent Lady Chapel providing a sense of what is still to come elsewhere.

The arrival of Manquehue in the UK has much the same feel. Drawing deeply on the roots of the Benedictine tradition and learning a great deal from the example set by Ampleforth, José Manuel brought the Benedictine renewal he had helped establish in Chile back to the English monasteries that had first inspired him. The past has not been swept away but the tradition is being renewed. In this context, it is worth noting that books recommended to Manquehue Oblates in Chile include *Spiritual Friendship* by St Aelred of Rievaulx and the *Life of St Benedict* by St Gregory the Great, in addition to the Rule of St Benedict and the Sacred Scriptures. At a time when introductory reading for most Catholics rarely stretches back past the 1960s, this is a bold statement of faith in the continuity of the Faith, a real hermeneutic of continuity in action.

What I saw when I first met the small Chilean community that had been established at Ampleforth was, therefore, the end of a very long process. What I had stumbled upon was an ongoing pilgrimage, which I was now invited to join. We tend to think of pilgrimages as single journeys. We set off from home towards a holy site and then return home afterwards. The reality is much more complex. All pilgrimages are journeys that are, in fact, responses to previous journeys. In setting off for Rome, we are responding to the great apostolic journeys that Saints Paul and Peter made many years before. We can only go on pilgrimage to Santiago de Compostela because St James went there before us. Even traveling to Lourdes is an acknowledgement that St Bernadette had first gone on her own spiritual journey, which itself brought millions of pilgrims to the grotto where she met Our Lady. In making our own pilgrimage to Ampleforth at Easter, we joined hundreds of other pilgrims and a small group of Chileans, whose own pilgrimage had consisted of crisscrossing the world in response to a simple call heard in the course of *lectio divina*.

## Spiritual friendship

Returning home from Ampleforth, I got back in touch with someone I knew from my daughter's school. Having been educated herself in one of the Manquehue schools in Chile, she invited me to the *lectio divina* group she and her husband held at their house and taught me a great deal more about the work of the movement. Having been educated at San Benito's, she was an enthusiastic witness to the long-term benefits the movement has brought. Her husband, who had been educated at Ampleforth and spent some time in Chile as a *gringo*, also testified to the life-changing nature of the Manquehue approach. There is nothing extraordinary about their situation—they work hard at home and at work and are committed members of the local parish—except for the fact that their lives have been shaped by the Manquehue movement and are grounded in the practice of *lectio divina*.

What was it, I wanted to know, that was distinctive about Manquehue? What had made a difference to them? The simple answer to both questions was the Manquehue commitment to spiritual friendship. Having *tutoría* at the heart of the Manquehue school experience had clearly made a huge impact on them both and so, on their return to the UK, they had looked for ways to develop what they had learned. The long-term aim among former *gringos* was to set up a Manquehue school in Britain, but when that plan didn't come to fruition they formed the Community of St Aelred instead, drawing on the work and inspiration of the twelfth-century Cistercian monk. Though dispersed throughout the country, members of the community commit themselves to the spiritual friendship of which St Aelred wrote. That is why we saw them at Ampleforth each year and that is also why we bumped into them as we stepped out of the tent at Youth 2000. No longer restricted to just one city in South America, the Manquehue movement was making its presence felt across the globe.

Here, then, was another model of community. In moving to the UK, the Manquehue movement had changed and adapted. Could this be a model for others to follow? I wondered. Would it remain content to be an essentially Chilean community that has links with the UK and a few other countries, or would it become a regular sight in the universal Church? I wasn't sure and my friends weren't sure either. For the time being, I had to be content with the limited exposure I had to this lay community that was in the world without being of the world, but I wasn't entirely content. Impressed by what I had seen, I was now keen to find other examples of radical Christianity in action. It was time to move on.

# 5

# Opus Dei

**B**EFORE LEAVING the Franciscans of the Renewal in London, I said a prayer before their collection of relics, one of which, to my surprise, was a set of rosary beads that had belonged to St Josémaria Escriva, the Spanish founder of Opus Dei. This took me aback because I had never made a link between these two, apparently very different, groups.

My first experience of Opus Dei was, appropriately enough, in Spain. A former work colleague invited me and another colleague to join him on what he considered a pilgrimage to Santiago de Compostela but what I thought of as a cycling holiday in Northern Spain. I was not a Catholic then and had no understanding of what a pilgrimage was, so, rather than prepare for a spiritual journey, I bought myself a touring bike, launched into a training regime, and looked forward to our half-term trip.

The problems began before we even left the UK. I was living in the fens of rural Cambridgeshire at the time and so any cycling I did in preparation for my holiday was on the flattest ground that England has to offer. Even so, I thought my new bike a little on the heavy side and wondered if I should have chosen something a little less robust. Thrusting such concerns to one side, I asked my colleague, who was originally from Spain, whether there was anything else I needed to do to prepare. He said that he was happy for me to leave the planning and preparation to him, though he did suggest that we should perhaps deflate our tires before loading our bikes onto the plane in case they popped with the change of pressure. We duly took this advice but it wasn't until we arrived in Spain that we realized that none of us had brought along a bike pump. As a result, we spent two hours in Burgos trying to get the bikes roadworthy

## Opus Dei

again while a group of old men watched us with undisguised interest. Eventually one of them found us a pump that worked and we struggled on to our first stop several hours behind schedule.

I recently found a few scrawled comments in a notebook I took with me on that trip. Some of them are enigmatic: *yellow signs—trusted—official signs not*. Others have poetic pretensions: *old Spanish men with Audenesque faces and berets*. Others are bafflingly incomplete: *tea and marg & caramel chocolates*. What comes through loud and clear, though, is that I didn't have a great time, even after we got our bikes fixed. I described what I missed (*tea and BBC Radio*), I described the weather (*wet with no chance to get dry*), and I complained about the *refugios*, the pilgrim hostels (*lack of central heating a shock*). Above all else, I expressed my utter bewilderment at the Catholicism I encountered. On visiting León Museum, I claimed that *Catholic ornaments make more sense in a museum than in a church*. On hearing some nuns singing, I wrote: *one small, one tall, one old, one fabulously old*, adding that they were *singing a quarter tone apart from the organ* in a way that reminded me of one of George Benjamin's modernist pieces. And in Mosteiro de San Paolo de Antealtares, I sounded downright petty, commenting that I was *sick of the sight of more religion*.

Not even the cathedral at Santiago de Compostela was able to move me. I complained about having to queue to get in, about the lack of atmosphere, about five priests chatting at the front, and about the crowds wandering around making no attempt to keep quiet. I also showed very few signs of curiosity: *down steps to something—tomb of St J? Up steps—long queue to something—tomb of St J—a real sprawl of a cathedral—pissing down with rain*. Some of the most significant moments in my Catholic life have come on pilgrimages, so I look back in amazement at the bad-tempered displeasure I poured into my notebook in those pre-Catholic days. Things got so bad, I even started to write a poem to express my annoyance. Its title was "A Very Twentieth-Century Pilgrim" and it is incomplete. Nonetheless, its very disjointedness conveys something of the confusion I felt at the time:

## Travels in Radical Christianity

*Above Astorga*

the river runs red with mud
...
the moon is making this silence
...
I tilted at the lilting hills
...
a verse to exercise
and a Protestant to boot
...
I entered Santiago
by train
at night
and only half awake
vaguely wondering what it would be like
if only one believed.

That last section at least was true. I was full of doubt and I really did enter Santiago by train, having given up on cycling halfway through the journey, having realized that my flatland training had failed to prepare me for the steep Spanish hills. Leaving my colleagues to battle on, I hopped onto a train and settled down with a battered copy of Dostoevsky's *Crime and Punishment* to cheer myself up. Eventually we all met again in Santiago, but by then I had resolved never to go on a cycling holiday again.

This was the context in which I first came across Opus Dei. Flying into Bilbao, we were met by friends of my colleague who put our bikes into the back of their minibus and took us up into the hills to visit the Opus Dei school where they worked, rather than into Bilbao itself so we could visit the Guggenheim Museum of Modern Art, as I had hoped. The school, to my uneducated eyes, looked much like any other school, but I may not have looked that closely because I was feeling disgruntled: I was on holiday and the last place I wanted to visit was somewhere that reminded me of work. After a lengthy visit to the school, we eventually set off along the pilgrimage route on our bikes, eventually arriving at the Opus Dei house in Santiago. Again, I showed remarkably little curiosity about the establishment, though I did join the others in watching the film they were showing that evening: *The Prince of Egypt*, an animated version of the story of Moses. I was mildly baffled by why adults should choose to watch an animated film but no longer had the energy to give it any sustained thought.

Taking my annoyance with me the next day, I steadfastly refused to visit the tomb of Saint Iago himself. Such superstitious attachment to the remains of someone who probably wasn't St James anyway was not for the likes of a Protestant like me. Looking back, I now wonder what on earth I was doing but, at the time, I turned away from Santiago with relief. Shortly after my return to the UK, I got a new job and lost contact with my former colleague. I also obliterated Santiago de Compostela, cycling holidays in Spain, and Opus Dei from my mind.

**Parents as primary educators**
Years later, two events brought Opus Dei back into view. The first was the furor around Dan Brown's *The Da Vinci Code*. I was a Catholic by that point and thought I ought to read it. I did try but I never managed to finish it. Whatever its theological failings—and I am sure there were many—it was its literary weaknesses that really bothered me. More significant in my rediscovery of Opus Dei was a chance remark from my wife as we were struggling to find a suitable school for our daughter. There was an Opus Dei primary school nearby, she told me; perhaps we ought to have a look. Having only the haziest of ideas about what an Opus Dei school might look like in the UK, and still bearing the emotional scars from that unhappy holiday to Spain, I reluctantly agreed to attend an open day.

Just like the school I visited in Spain, the one we visited in London was, on the face of it, entirely ordinary. Primary school classrooms are much the same the world over: they have tiny desks and chairs; their walls are festooned with brightly colored displays; they are jam-packed with engaging activities for little hands. There was nothing distinctive about the building itself, but what made the place stand out were the people we talked to as we went round. Not just the paid staff—the headmaster and the teachers—but the parent volunteers who had given up their Saturday mornings to be there.

A long conversation with a local doctor made a particular impression on me. He explained that the purpose of the school was to assist parents in the job of educating our children. Parents are the primary educators, he said, gently introducing me to a fundamental teaching of the Church that had somehow passed me by, even though I had been a teacher for twenty years and a Catholic for ten years by that stage. It is not the job of schools to take that primary duty away from parents—we don't simply cede control of our children the moment they put on a school uniform for the first time—but to enhance it. Schools are there to support parents in what can sometimes be trying circumstances, and they are there to teach, but parents remain the first educators, the ones from whom their children learn most.

That conversation turned my view of education upside down. It also gave me great confidence. What had been a nagging uncertainty suddenly became the key issue for us as we made important decisions about our daughter's future. We knew her better than anyone else and were reluctant to send her to a school that treated her like a cog in a machine, knowing that this is the main problem with our educational system today: it is built on an industrial model and assumes that with the right, standardized input, the correct output will result. We weren't interested in output or in any of the other industrial paraphernalia that goes with it: quality assurance, regular testing, independent inspections. What we wanted was an education that took our daughter seriously as a person, and in that little school in an unpretentious corner of south London we found what we were looking for.

Moving house to be closer to the school, we discovered that we were not alone. Several other families in the neighborhood had done the same, some of them moving very long distances. What was it about the place, we wondered, that inspired such commitment? Gradually, as we became immersed in the life of the school, we began to understand. Over time, the spirituality and slightly arcane structure of Opus Dei became clearer to us. Though Opus Dei has its own priests, about 98% of Opus Dei members are laypeople and the vast majority of them, known as supernumeraries, are married people who live in the world while following the path set out by St Josémaria Escriva. Along with the priests and the numeraries—laypeople who have devoted themselves to celibacy and who generally live in Opus Dei centers—they attend weekly and monthly meetings, a yearly retreat, and a formation course. All members of Opus Dei attend Mass daily and commit themselves to prayer, including the rosary, and Bible reading. The members we met were clearly good people who loved the Church and were keen to live out their vocation in the world with great faithfulness.

## The universal call to holiness

This work in the world is important. At the heart of Opus Dei is the idea that everyone can attain holiness in their everyday lives, which is why no distinction is made between the lay and ordained members of the organization. St Josémaria once wrote that God "calls each and every one to holiness; He asks each and every one to love him: young and old, single and married, healthy and sick, learned and unlearned, no matter where they work, or where they are." In that sense, Opus Dei's key message is no different from the one that has been preached by saints throughout the ages. The universal call to holiness is a fundamental aspect of the Christian message. However, St Josémaria emphasized one aspect of this universal call: the importance of serving God in and through our everyday activities and especially through our work. Again this was not an entirely new message. St John Vianney, the Curé of Ars, once told his congregation: "Oh, how we could merit heaven every day, my dear brethren, by doing just our ordinary duties, but by doing them for God and the salvation of our souls!" He then explained that if "you work with the object of pleasing God and obeying His Commandments, which order you to earn your bread by the sweat of your brow, that is an act of obedience [to God]."

Finding God "in the midst of the realities and interests of the world" also lies at the heart of Opus Dei's spirituality. According to St Josémaria, the route we follow through life may be unspectacularly ordinary, but that doesn't make it any less treacherous, since the "danger lies in routine, in imagining that God cannot be here, in the things of each instant, because they are so simple and ordinary!" Because God is in the everyday events, we have no choice but to sanctify our daily work. Not to do so would be to fall into a dualist trap that suggests that the material world is entirely divorced from the spiritual one. The sanctification of work, for St Josémaria, is therefore "the hinge of true spirituality for people who, like us, have decided to come close to God while being at the same time fully involved in temporal affairs." He also explained that our "ordinary activities are not an insignificant matter. Rather they are the very hinge on which our sanctity turns, and offer us constant opportunities of meeting God, and of praising Him and glorifying Him through our intellectual or manual work." The radicalism of Opus Dei consists in its refusal to be radical, in its relentless focus on the sanctification of everyday life: what St Josémaria wanted was a change of emphasis rather than a change of direction.

Most institutions associated with Opus Dei blend into the world around them. Schools tend to be given names like The Heights, The Willows Academy, or Montrose School rather than St Benedict's, St Teresa's, or St Joseph's, while Opus Dei houses of residence are usually named after local places: Hillcrest; Kelston; Netherhall. The interior design of these schools and residences is also quite different from many older Catholic institutions. There tends to be relatively little religious art on the walls—in this way, at least, Opus Dei's practice is similar to that of the Bruderhof—though there is always a chapel or oratory. Opus Dei youth clubs also stand out by not standing out. Ordinary activities—games, crafts, drama—are the means by which children are drawn closer to God. How does this work? St Josémaria expressed it clearly when he said that "Human virtues constitute the foundation for the supernatural virtues." If we learn to be diligent, prudent, courageous and so on, we will find ourselves on the path to holiness. "Our heads should indeed be touching heaven, but our feet should be firmly on the ground."

### Deepening prayer

A crucial aspect of St Josémaria's approach to the Christian vocation is his understanding of prayer. In his wonderful book on prayer, Simon Tugwell O.P. explains, "in our relationship with God, one of the main problems is that half the time we just forget about it. We may have the most beautiful and edifying thoughts during our morning prayers, and whole new vistas of Christian life may from time to time open out before us, but yet when it actually comes to the practical crunch, it just seems to slip out of our minds. And at the end of the day we kick ourselves for having been just as unforgiving, uninspiring, unregenerate, as ever." Tugwell suggests, therefore, that "somehow we must find a way of remembering God that does not work in fits and starts, but that will actually last through the day," explaining that meditation "is not primarily a matter of spending a certain period of time every now and then having beautiful thoughts, but about building up a Christian memory." St Josémaria made strikingly similar points, telling his followers that a "Christian life should be one of constant prayer, trying to live in the presence of God from morning to night and from night to morning," and that while "being fully involved in his everyday work, among other men, his equals; busy, under stress, the Christian has to be at the same time totally involved with God, for he is a child of God." How is that possible? How is it possible to be both busy at work— "under stress" —and to live constantly in the presence of God? According to St Josémaria, there are two connected answers. Like Simon Tugwell, he suggests that Christians commit themselves to traditional Catholic devotions and meditation:

> Try to commit yourself to a plan of life and to keep to it: a few minutes of mental prayer, Holy Mass—daily, if you can manage it—and frequent Communion; regular recourse to the Holy Sacrament of Forgiveness—even though your conscience does not accuse you of mortal sin; visiting Jesus in the Tabernacle; praying and contemplating the mysteries of the Holy Rosary, and so many other marvelous devotions you know or can learn.

This plan of life might sound daunting, but St Josémaria goes out of his way to emphasize that it should not be allowed to become a set of rigid rules. He also explains that "the important thing does not lie in doing many things," suggesting instead that his readers should "limit yourself, generously, to those that you can fulfil each day." The inevitable consequence of such an approach will be that these practices "will lead you, almost without your realizing it, to contemplative prayer" and that "this will happen while you go about your ordinary duties, when you answer the telephone, get on a bus, open or close a door, pass in front of a church, when you begin a new task, during it and when you have finished it: you will find yourself referring everything you do to your Father God."

The second part of his answer to the question of how we can live constantly in the presence of God lies in our turning "work into prayer," remembering that an "hour of study, for a modern apostle, is an hour of prayer." If prayer is the raising of the heart and mind to God—and if the heart, as the Catechism teaches, is "the depths of one's being, where the person decides for or against God"—then we pray with actions as well as with words, both consciously and subconsciously. That is why St Josémaria, anticipating the Manquehue movement, was unequivocal about the fact that we need to be "contemplatives in the middle of the world." That is why he said that "prayer becomes continuous, like the beating of our heart, like our pulse," adding that "without this presence of God, there is no contemplative life, our working for Christ is worth very little, for vain is the builder's toil if the house is not of the Lord's building."

Although members of Opus Dei tend to call the organization "the Work," it is not, strictly speaking, work that lies at the heart of Opus Dei's spirituality. St Josémaria may have adapted St Benedict's ideas about the work of God for a twentieth-century secular context, but he put the notion of divine filiation—the truth that we are all children of God—at the core of Opus Dei's spirituality. It could also be argued that a profound, if largely implicit, understanding of the human heart is central to the spirituality of Opus Dei, St Josémaria's teaching about prayer and work drawing on considerations perhaps best expressed in these beautiful words from the Catechism:

> The heart is the dwelling-place where I am, where I live; according to the Semitic or biblical expression, the heart is the place "to which I withdraw." The heart is our hidden center, beyond the grasp of our reason and of others; only the Spirit of God can fathom the human heart and know it fully. The heart is the place of decision, deeper than our psychic drives. It is the place of

truth, where we choose life or death. It is the place of encounter, because as image of God we live in relation: it is the place of covenant.

If this is what the heart is then there are profound implications for how we understand prayer and how, in particular, we can pray in the everyday events of life: "One cannot always meditate, but one can always enter into inner prayer, independently of the conditions of health, work, or emotional state. The heart is the place of this quest and encounter, in poverty and in faith." Or, to use St Josémaria's words:

> God is interested even in the smallest events in the lives of his creatures—in your affairs and mine—and He calls each of us by our name. This certainty which the faith gives enables us to look at everything in a new light. And everything, while remaining exactly the same, becomes different, because it is an expression of God's love. Our life is turned into a continuous prayer, we find ourselves with good humor and a peace which never ends, and everything we do is an act of thanksgiving running through all our day.

**Becoming holy through work**

I was given the opportunity to experience this approach to prayer several years after first visiting the little primary school in London when a group of Opus Dei families decided to expand their educational work by opening two high schools. When the headmaster of The Cedars, the boys' school that was being planned for South London, approached me to see if I was interested in working with him, I suddenly had to make a big decision. Should I leave my comfortable job and throw in my lot with a project that was still very much up in the air, or should I stick with the work with which I was familiar? A building had been found for the school but it needed extensive renovation; a senior management team was in place (including my former colleague who had arranged the cycling pilgrimage to Santiago de Compostela) but there were neither teachers nor students; the school was a vision, but a huge amount of work was still needed if that vision was to become a reality. Excitement at the opportunity

*Travels in Radical Christianity*

I had been offered was mixed with nerves about the practical problems, so, after much thought and probably not nearly enough prayer, I kept one foot in my current job and joined the new school as part-time Director of Learning. Many months later, after a lot of meetings, a great deal of building work, and some practical setbacks, the school opened with just twenty-four students.

Work may be theologically important but it is not always glamorous. In fact, it is often a slog, which is why people often long to be rid of it. That first year of the school's existence was hard work. Everything had to be created from scratch. There were no resources to fall back on. Meetings proliferated as we plotted our way through the year. Nonetheless, the school not only survived but grew. We had planned to take on an extra year group each year, but when a group of families asked us to take on their older children too, we couldn't refuse and so the expansion accelerated, albeit from a very small base. Keeping our heads down as we got on with the job, it was hard to see the bigger picture, but slowly that picture emerged. The school now has a full complement of students aged 11 to 18 and has outgrown the original premises.

What we were trying to achieve at the school was summed up beautifully by the chaplain when he preached at a start-of-term Mass. Recalling the foundation of the University of Navarre in 1952, he told the story of the day the founder showed St Josémaria around. "This is it," he said with justifiable pride, for the creation of a university from scratch is no small matter. "This is the university you asked me to found." To his surprise St Josémaria corrected him. "I didn't tell you to found a university," he said. "I told you to become holy by founding a university." In the same way, our task is to become holy through our work—to become saints through the things we do in our everyday lives—not to achieve goals, however commendable those goals might be in themselves. In a sense, this is an obvious message, but it is also revolutionary. I have worked in many schools, but in all the many meetings I have attended over the years I had never before been told that my job was to become holy through the work I did that term.

The work we were doing was clearly important, but I also had a clear sense that work could itself become a problem. If, as St Josémaria once wrote, "work is the vehicle through which each person is inserted into society, the means by which we find a place in the ensemble of human relationships, the instrument for assigning us a position, a place in human society," wasn't there a danger that work would tend to displace family life and social relations? If the sanctification of work became the "hinge of true spirituality," wasn't it likely in our work-obsessed society that we would give too much time to work, with the inevitable result that our families would be neglected to some degree? The obvious answer to these worries was to adopt John Ruskin's position: "Now in order that people may be happy in their work, these three things are needed: They must be fit for it: They must not do too much of it: and they must have a sense of success in it." The problem was that I wasn't sure how much work was too much, and I also suspected that Ruskin's beautiful phrasing was masking a mis-directed question. In order to resolve my uncertainty, I decided to set out on another journey, to visit the headquarters of Opus Dei in the United Kingdom.

**Visiting headquarters**
Orme Court is situated in a very pleasant area of central London, close to Hyde Park and Kensington Palace. It doesn't stand out from the street, though. In fact, I walked straight past it and had to backtrack. Looking closely, I found a tiny label on the doorbell that told me I had arrived. I rang the bell and wondered what sort of place I would find inside.

What struck me immediately was that there was nothing corporate about the Opus Dei headquarters. It looked like what it had once been: a beautiful house in a lovely part of the capital. The presence of St Josémaria was obvious throughout the house: his portrait, a relic, a painting he had given to the people who set up Opus Dei in the United Kingdom. Opus Dei very much revolves around the life and teachings of its founder, as is the case with most religious communities, which is one reason Opus Dei is so difficult to categorize: this quintessentially lay movement was founded, and continues to be inspired by, a priest; it is an organization that embodies a vision of the Christian life that was expressed at the Second Vatican Council, though it was founded many years earlier; it is a modern institution that keeps the traditional religious orders at arm's length, and yet its members endeavor to follow traditional Church teaching.

My host for the afternoon was Pablo, an extremely jolly numerary whom I had first met five years previously and who was now the National Youth Director. It wouldn't take much of a leap to imagine Pablo as a Franciscan Friar of the Renewal—he has the same enthusiasm for life and the same infectious joy in whatever he does—but Pablo's vocation was not to become a friar but to live out his life of service as a layman in the world. The tour of Orme Court was fascinating but more interesting still was the conversation we had about work that afternoon. Pablo was refreshingly honest—as well as relentlessly cheerful—about the work of Opus Dei, pointing out that it is still a young organization that will undoubtedly develop further over time. We talked about many topics, but the one our conversation kept returning to was the nature of work itself, because I wanted to know whether there was a recognition in Opus Dei that work could become overwhelming and so lead people away from God.

To help me with my questions, Pablo sent me some material to read. One document in particular set out to explain the image of the hinge that St Josémaria repeatedly used. It pointed out that work can only be a hinge when it is attached to something. Just as a door is useless unless it is attached by hinges to a wall, so too does work only find its meaning when it is attached to something else, most importantly family life and social relations:

> The sanctification of professional work (together with the sanctification of family and social life) is not only essential in order to shape society in accord with God's will, but it forms the "hinge" in the tapestry that these three aspects make up. It is not that professional duties are *more important* than family and social tasks, but rather that they serve as a support for the family and for social cohesion. The importance or priority of a duty depends on the order of charity, not on whether it is a professional, social or family duty.

That got right to the nub of the matter. It helped me see that work is not the be-all-and-end-all for Opus Dei but also explained why work nonetheless holds such a special place in the organization's spirituality. The same document also set out St Josémaria's view that our professional vocation is part of our divine vocation "in so far as it is a means for attaining sanctity and for helping others to do so." The caveat is important, so important, in fact, that St Josémaria went on to explain that "if at any point the professional vocation were to become an obstacle . . . if it absorbs one to such an extent that it impedes interior life or the faithful fulfilment of one's duties of state . . . it is not part of the divine vocation, because it is no longer a professional vocation." The founder of Opus Dei was quite certain that there is an end to work.

Having traveled to Spain and returned to England before setting out on another journey to learn about the work of Opus Dei, I felt as though my travels were beginning to get me somewhere. As I visited different communities, I was starting to see the richness of radical, counter-cultural Christianity in action, to appreciate that there is more than one way of fruitfully challenging the status quo. However, I also knew that I still had a long way to go because I still had many questions that had not been answered. Having experienced work with Opus Dei, it made sense to explore the same theme with a quite different group of radical Christians. I was off to visit members of the Catholic Worker Movement.

# 6

# The Catholic Worker Movement

AS THE NUMBER 29 BUS lumbered slowly through Haringay in North London, I gradually became aware of a persistent noise. A convoy of cars was slowly gaining on us, each one blaring its horns. At first, I assumed that this must be normal behavior in North London, but when my fellow passengers started to voice their disapproval, I realized that something else was going on. As we pulled up to our stop, the convoy swept past us, a lone and unidentifiable flag flying from the final car's window. Celebration or protest? No one seemed sure.

Turning off the main road, where a Halal restaurant sat cheek by jowl with a betting shop, I walked along a row of terrace houses. In one window, I saw a Ukrainian flag with *No War* written across it. In another, a Black Lives Matter poster. Further uphill, I saw a large church. A decommissioned church, it turned out. But next door was the place I had been looking for: Giuseppe Conlon House, the headquarters of the London Catholic Worker Movement.

The Catholic Worker Movement was founded, and still has its strongest presence, in the USA. Its founders, Dorothy Day and Peter Maurin, began their project with a newspaper which they sold in New York City, but their longer-term aims were much bolder, as Dorothy Day explained in her autobiography, *The Long Loneliness*:

> [Peter] wished to give me a Catholic outline of history—but he also wished to repeat over and over again his program of action: round-table discussions, house of hospitality and agronomic universities. We were to popularize this program for immediate

needs, which in itself would be the seed for a long-range program, a green revolution, by publishing a paper for the man in the street.

Such a program found a ready audience in the 1930s, and Peter Maurin was shrewd enough to realize that Dorothy Day was the right person to drive it through. The sister and daughter of journalists and a radical journalist herself, she immediately saw the need for such a paper, though she worried about the practicalities. Where were they going to start? Who was going to fund it? Peter Maurin tended not to worry about such prosaic issues: "In the history of the saints," he said, "capital was raised by prayer. God sends you what you need when you need it." Maurin's heroes were saints like Francis de Sales, who "scattered leaflets like any radical," and St John of God, "who sold newspapers on the streets." He believed that it was entirely possible "to change the hearts and minds of men" as long as you put the truth to them. Truth and a vision of the future, for what he wanted above all was "to give [his readers] vision—the vision of a society where it is easier for men to be good." He soon convinced Dorothy Day to work with him, though they couldn't agree on the name of their publication. "He wanted to call the paper *The Catholic Radical*," she later wrote, "but with my Communist background, I insisted on calling it *The Catholic Worker*." And so the movement began.

### The labor problem

I was welcomed into Giuseppe Conlon House by Fr Martin Newell, who led me into a back room of the decommissioned church where lunch was being prepared. It wasn't his turn on the rota, so we chatted while the final preparations were being made. "Catholic and Worker: both words worry people," he told me. In post-Protestant Britain, there is still a certain amount of residual suspicion of Catholics, and "worker" sounds uncomfortably communist, so the combination of the two words gives the Catholic Worker Movement something of an image problem. Not that Fr Martin was too worried about image. He was quite happy to describe the movement to me as a group of Catholic pacifists and communitarian anarchists. No wonder, then, that getting past the language is one of the greatest challenges the movement faces to this day.

*Travels in Radical Christianity*

The idea of a Catholic Worker may have negative connotations, but work itself is very much back on the political agenda. Just a few days before my visit, I attended a lecture by the respected British MP Jon Cruddas about the dignity of work. In his talk, Cruddas argued that work is back on the political agenda for four main reasons. First, the pandemic, when work literally stopped, a "tiny virus redefined the role of the state," and "the value attached to the work of others—especially the vocations—the callings—of public service workers increased significantly." Second, the unprecedented productivity crisis through which we are currently passing. Third, "the recent waves of strikes and militancy that we've been living through." And fourth, the question of automation, which has prompted two very different responses: "One signposts a post-work nightmare of escalating inequality amongst a threatened humanity, subservient to technology. But the other, more popular view suggests a future utopia of abundance, numerous routes to self-actualization, and even enhanced transhuman possibilities." The worry here, Cruddas argued, was that "today few ethical questions are asked about technological change—we tend to shrink the conversation down to utilitarian concerns about what is best for Britain plc, rather than some of the deeper questions."

If Cruddas is right about the political significance of the labor question today, then we could do a lot worse than turn to Catholic Social Teaching for answers, as he did in his talk. We could also ask whether Dorothy Day and Peter Maurin can help us too. As I prepared for my visit, I returned to Day's autobiography, finding this intriguing passage about the worker: "We used the word in its broadest sense, meaning those who worked with hand or brain, those who did physical, mental or spiritual work. But we thought primarily of the poor, the dispossessed, the exploited." Her definition was both wider and more specific than I had remembered, but it was the more specific definition, workers as poor, dispossessed, and exploited, that mattered most to her:

> Every one of us who was attracted to the poor had a sense of guilt, of responsibility, a feeling that in some way we were living on the labor of others. The fact that we were born in a certain environ-

ment, were enabled to go to school, were endowed with the ability to compete with others and hold our own, that we had few physical disabilities—all these things marked us as the privileged in a way. We felt a respect for the poor and destitute as those nearest to God, as those chosen by Christ for his compassion.

Questions of work and poverty were always entwined for Dorothy Day, which perhaps explains why she approvingly quoted the words of William James in one of his essays:

> Poverty is indeed the strenuous life,—without brass bands or uniforms or hysteric popular applause or lies or circumlocutions; and when one sees the way in which wealth-getting enters as an ideal into the very bone and marrow of our generation, one wonders whether the revival of the belief that poverty is a worthy religious vocation may not be the transformation of military courage, and the spiritual reform which our time stands most in need of.

This understanding of the importance of poverty takes us a step further: for Dorothy Day, work, poverty, and spiritual reform all went together. Having turned away from godless communism, she argued strenuously that Catholics could only pursue their true mission when they embraced poverty as a vocation and worked for the common good of all, but most of all for the poor and dispossessed.

### Community, hospitality, resistance

There was a certain irony in the fact that Fr Martin and I were chatting in a building which was no longer being used for the purpose for which it had been built, which no longer worked as it was meant to be. Built as a Methodist church, it had been taken over by the Catholic Diocese of Westminster only to close its doors as a church in the early 2000s. A couple of years later, the diocese offered it to the Catholic Worker Movement, which used it at first as a community house and emergency night shelter, some twenty men sleeping on mattresses on the floor of what had once been the church hall. Gradually they upgraded the building, providing shared bedrooms to replace the mattresses on the floor. Then Covid hit. Five men remained in the building, staying in their own bedrooms, while the rest of the guests moved to hotels. It was a difficult time for those who stayed and for those who left. With the Covid crisis over, the community is gradually building up again. When I visited, there were ten guests in their own bedrooms and hopes that more space could be converted.

Catholic Workers may be described as Catholic pacifists and communitarian anarchists, but another approach, Fr Martin told me, is to think about the three pillars of their work: community, hospitality, and resistance. We can respond to our fractured and atomized world, the Catholic Worker Movement believes, by rebuilding community in very practical ways, starting with those who are prepared to dedicate themselves to such a counter-cultural lifestyle. Of the five people who currently form the house's permanent community, three work full-time for the movement while one works in a local hospital and another works for the diocese. All are volunteers who contribute their time and money as they can, especially if they have paid employment outside the community. In the past the community consisted of Anglicans, Quakers, Methodists, and atheists, as well as Catholics. Now all the members are Catholic.

With a strong community in place, the second pillar—hospitality—can be built. Peter Maurin's vision of houses of hospitality as a response to the Great Depression in '30s America is now instantiated in a home which welcomes destitute asylum seekers who have "no recourse to public funds," to use the government jargon. When the Catholic Worker Movement arrived in London at the start of the millennium, there was very little provision in the UK for these destitute asylum seekers, so it seemed an obvious place to start. Since the Syrian refugee crisis, more provision has been made but the problem has also got worse, those who arrive at Giuseppe Conlon House coming predominantly from Africa and the Middle East.

The third and final pillar is resistance, and that is what most clearly sets the Catholic Worker Movement apart from the other groups I had visited. Dorothy Day may have left atheistic communism behind when she founded the Catholic Worker Movement, but she still believed in the importance of non-violent direct action when justice demanded it. Fr Martin clearly held much the same belief and had the prison record to prove it. His first and longest stint in prison was six months for criminal damage and burglary, though burglary is a curious description of an attempt to decommission a nuclear-weapons convoy by hammering on it.

Why did he do it? I asked. Was he looking to be arrested, or were his arrest and imprisonment simply an unfortunate side effect of his activism? Fr Martin first told me about the crime itself, explaining that it was a symbolic and literal attempt to disarm major weapons systems; his aim was to beat hammers into ploughshares. Then he reflected on his imprisonment. To my surprise, he said that it was an opportunity to see faith and life in the world from another angle. In prison, he became one of the dispossessed. I wondered if this was to romanticize imprisonment, but Fr Martin soon convinced me that this was not the case. He was disarmingly frank about the realities of prison life, while also being keen not to exaggerate the difficulties he had faced. For a start, he said, most of his stints in prison, with the exception of that first occasion, had been short, lasting from just under two days to two weeks. He had spent time in Bedford and Belmarsh on remand, and ended up in Pentonville, Brixton, and Wandsworth Prisons on a couple of occasions each. There was always a fear of violence in the air in prison, he told me, though he never actually saw any violence: "I heard it," he said, "but I didn't see it." Other difficulties included sensory deprivation and the challenge of living in a very physically restricted environment, though his worst experience seems to have been sharing a cell with a prisoner who kept the TV on until 2 am each day. Prisons are the new monasteries, Catholic Worker activists were fond of saying in the 1950s, but there's not much monastic silence in jail.

The more he talked the less romantic it sounded, especially when he told me that he sometimes had to warn psychologically vulnerable activists not to risk arrest because life in prison is so difficult. "I had to work hard to stay OK," he said, adding that "staying OK" came to be his main work in prison, though he did also have "a kind of ministry" when he shared a cell with a vulnerable cellmate. Being in prison clearly wasn't an experience he relished, and it is perhaps significant that, while members of the community do still take part in direct action, their focus has shifted noticeably from activism to hospitality in recent years. Nonetheless, Fr Martin's description of his resistance work and his time in prison did raise numerous questions. Putting it bluntly, was this aspect of the Catholic Worker Movement's work something I could endorse? As a father, how would I feel if my children got involved in direct action? In short, what did I think of anarchy?

### The Anarchists' Book Fair

While researching the Catholic Worker Movement, I stumbled across the London Anarchist Book Fair, a curious event which this year hosted stalls run by, among others, Angry Workers, Antiuniversity Now, Art for Animals, Critisticuffs, Earth First, Feminist Fightback, the Left Book Club, Palestine Action, RS21 (Revolutionary Socialism in the Twenty-First Century), Seditionist Distribution, and Transgender Action Block. In the early 2000s, the London Catholic Worker tried to book a stall at the fair but was turned down because anarchism was deemed to be "irreconcilable with an 'authoritarian' Roman Catholic Church." Eventually a resolution was reached: "After some sharp exchanges, we were given a space, and it is a credit to the organizers that they were willing to listen and change their minds," a writer in *The London Catholic Worker* opined. However, that wasn't quite the end of the story. In 2017 the book fair made national headlines when what the organizers called "a confrontation" took place, "sparked by two people handing out anti-trans leaflets, and a subsequent online firestorm." After a protracted furor, the 2018 book fair was cancelled and recriminations rang out on every side. I won't go into the details: they're not very edifying.

Most people reading headlines like "UK transgender rights row intensifies as book fair is cancelled" wouldn't have been that surprised. What else would you expect from a gathering of anarchists? The answer depends entirely on your understanding of anarchy, so I asked Fr Martin where he stood on the question. Why do Catholic Workers call themselves anarchists? Why do they embrace what appears to be such a disreputable philosophy? Why was Fr Martin still planning to attend, and possibly even to run a stall, at the 2023 anarchist book fair?

In answering those questions, Fr Martin suggested that there had been tension over the extent to which the Catholic Worker Move-

## The Catholic Worker Movement

ment was anarchist from the very beginning. Dorothy Day wasn't an anarchist, he said (at least, "she wasn't an anarchist unless she could be the Anarch"), but Peter Maurin was "a bit provocative," though even he tended to speak more about personalism than anarchism in later years. In fact, he sounded positively irenic at times. Here he is in a remarkably concise article about "What the Catholic Worker Believes," from his 1934 collection of "Easy Essays":

1. The Catholic Worker believes in the gentle personalism of traditional Catholicism.
2. The Catholic Worker believes in the personal obligation of looking after the needs of our brother and sister.
3. The Catholic Worker believes in the daily practice of the Works of Mercy.
4. The Catholic Worker believes in Houses of Hospitality for the immediate relief of those who are in need.
5. The Catholic Worker believes in the establishment of Farming Communes where each one works according to his ability and gets according to his need.
6. The Catholic Worker believes in creating a new society within the shell of the old with the philosophy of the new, which is not a new philosophy but a very old philosophy, a philosophy so old it looks like new.

Put like that, the aims of the Catholic Worker could be embraced by most Catholics, whatever their theological background. I found point six particularly intriguing because it takes a slogan from the preamble to the constitution of the IWW (Industrial Workers of the World) and tries to redeem it. Instead of the IWW's obviously militant manifesto—"It is the historic mission of the working class to do away with capitalism. The army of production must be organized, not only for everyday struggle with capitalists, but also to carry on production when capitalism shall have been overthrown. By organizing industrially we are forming the structure of the new society within the shell of the old"—we have something which sounds more like Pope Benedict XVI's hermeneutic of continuity.

Nonetheless, the fact remains that the Catholic Worker Movement does define itself as, in some way, anarchist, so what does that mean? Fr Martin, who is a gentle, soft-spoken man, explained that, in fact, they "weren't particularly focused on the anarchist bit." He then told me about a roundtable discussion the community had with a secular anarchist, who eventually came to the conclusion that Christian anarchism was a unique entity and not simply a quirky offshoot from the wider anarchist movement. "What it means for us," Fr Martin explained, "is that we follow God's laws rather than human laws."

That seemed simple enough, but I remembered an article in an old edition of *The London Catholic Worker* which suggested that the relationship between the Catholic movement and anarchism was rather more complex. In his article, Simon Watson started by drawing a useful distinction between anarchism and nihilism. "Many do not believe in building a new society within a shell of the old. They believe that the old must be destroyed first. That is nihilism." Fr Martin had said something similar, drawing a distinction between Catholic Workers and those secular anarchists who believe that "if you smash the government or capitalism, everything will be OK." By contrast, the Christian anarchist position, Simon Watson wrote, is that "the first government that must be brought down is the government of our own sins within ourselves." This revolution of the heart is the work of God and happens only when we bring all that is sinful within us to the foot of the cross. It turns secular anarchism on its head, which is why Watson is able to ask if it's possible to have real anarchism without Jesus Christ.

But what about the IWW slogan about building the new society in the shell of the old? Isn't that simply smuggling Marxist ideas into the Gospel? Not at all, Watson argued:

> The new social order is not created simply by trying to tear down [the trappings of the capitalist system] in a piecemeal and ineffectual way. Rather it comes about by the divine joy that flows in the simple acts of giving and receiving food, shelter, clothing, medicine, as well as giving our time to listen and encourage. It also arises from the prophetic word of truth spoken to those who persist in destructive behavior.... Out of these small individual acts, what St Thérèse of Lisieux calls the "little

# The Catholic Worker Movement

way," a great revolution takes place that little by little creates a whole new set of human-divine relationships that makes the cold and remote state system redundant.

Clearly the Catholic Worker Movement emerged out of, and still aligns itself with, the radical left, but it would be a mistake to see it as simply another political movement, a secular NGO with a Catholic tinge. It certainly draws on radical ideas, but those ideas are rooted more in the social teaching of the Church (and especially Pope Leo XIII's great encyclical *Rerum novarum*) than in the collected works of Karl Marx. That is why Fr Martin was keen to give me one final description of the Catholic Worker Movement: "Catholic Worker communities are built around the practice of the works of mercy and are based in houses of hospitality as places for the practice and organizing of works of mercy."

**We use it for prayer and storing stuff**
The Christian anarchism of the Catholic Worker Movement is not, I think, an issue which should concern too many Christians, but there is another aspect of the movement which nagged away at me during my visit. I have called my host Fr Martin but that is not what he called himself. He was Martin, and if I hadn't known he was a priest I might not have guessed. It was Sunday when we met, and he was wearing a pair of jeans and an open-topped checked shirt. I had wondered whether he would invite me to Mass with the community, but it transpired that they usually attend Mass in a local parish church. So I was slightly surprised to find, during a tour of the building, that the main body of the church is still functional, not least because the diocese has made that a requirement in case they ever want it back. I saw an altar and the tabernacle, though it no longer contained the Blessed Sacrament. What was the church's purpose, I wondered, if not for the celebration of Mass and the other sacraments? "We use it for prayer and storing stuff," Fr Martin told me. It wasn't a sentence I would ever have heard from a member of Opus Dei or a Franciscan Friar of the Renewal.

It was perhaps unsurprising, then, that Fr Martin expressed some discomfort at his position as a priest within the predominantly lay organization, admitting that his role was in some ways "anomalous." I asked him how he saw his own position in the community. "My role," he replied, "is building communities of disciples and discipleship." It's a commendable aim, but I still couldn't help thinking that his priesthood didn't seem to feature very prominently in the life of the community. As with the Bruderhof, something seemed to be missing, despite the manifestly good work the community was doing with destitute asylum seekers.

My unease seemed to be shared by some of the Catholic Workers. While Fr Martin spoke about the importance of having a non-hierarchical community, Simon Watson struggled adequately to answer the question that is sometimes thrown at the Catholic Worker Movement by secular anarchists: "How can a bona fide anarchist organization fit under the umbrella of the authoritarian Roman Catholic Church?" His first answer was that "Catholic Worker is not a Roman Catholic religious order and includes members from other denominations, other faiths, or even [those who] have no faith at all." He then pointed out that "in some quarters of the church [*sic*] the movement is unpopular and [to] some quarters of the movement the church is seen as irrelevant: the Atlanta Open Door Community describe themselves as the 'Protestant Catholic Worker': Boston Catholic Worker is mainly Buddhist."

However, realizing that he was largely dodging the question, he tried to pull the threads of his answer together: "Catholicism connects us to a religious body that upholds Christ and seeks to present the way in which we are to live according to God's will in a clear and unequivocal manner." While that may be true, there seems little here that is specifically Catholic, so he attempted further clarification: "Historically there may have been times when Christian anarchism and Catholicism could not [co-]exist. Today that isn't the case." Why? I want to ask. What has changed? Watson doesn't tell us, but he does drop the seeds of a solution to his conundrum into the final sentence of his article: "Today that isn't the case and Dorothy Day's vision of anarchist society with the structure and authority of the church in a supportive role is now more real than ever." I wasn't convinced that he'd squared the circle, but I also sensed that if there was an answer I needed to return to the writings of Dorothy Day to find it.

# The Catholic Worker Movement

In her autobiography, Day writes movingly about her conversion to Catholicism and its cost. Before she took that decisive step, she knew full well that the conversion she longed for would separate her from many friends and comrades on the Left. She also knew that it would mean an end to her common-law marriage, since her common-law husband wanted nothing to do with the Church, as he had shown when she had their baby baptized: "He had thought of the baptism only as a mumbo jumbo, the fuss and flurry peculiar to woman. At first he had been indulgent and had brought in the lobsters for the [baptism] feast. And then he had become angry with some sense of the end to which all this portended. Jealousy set in and he left me." Not yet a Catholic herself, Dorothy Day still could have backed away from the claims of the Church. But she didn't. She pressed on, leaving another love behind her:

> I speak of the misery of leaving one love. But there was another love too, the life I had led in the radical movement. That very winter I was writing a series of articles, interviews with the workers, with the unemployed. I was working with the Anti-Imperialist League, a Communist affiliate, that was bringing aid and comfort to the enemy, General Sandino's forces in Nicaragua. I was just as much against capitalism and imperialism as ever, and here I was going over to the opposition. . . .

So why did she do it? Because "I wanted to be poor, chaste and obedient. I wanted to die in order to live, to put off the old man and put on Christ. I loved, in other words, and like all women in love, I wanted to be united to my love." It was the overwhelming love of Christ which brought Dorothy Day into the Church and it was his love that enabled her, slowly and joylessly at first, to leave her old loves behind. The struggle continued long after her conversion, but what helped her become the saintly powerhouse that she eventually became was the sacraments of the Church. Reading *The Long Loneliness*, it is striking how often Day mentions going to confession. Here she is writing about Our Lady of Guadalupe Church in New York, where the faith which eventually gave rise to the Catholic Worker Movement was nourished:

*Travels in Radical Christianity*

> It was a narrow little church, served by the Augustinian Fathers of the Assumption, and there were Masses at seven, eight and nine o'clock each morning. Before every Mass priests came from the rectory next door to hear confessions. There were three confessionals on either side of the entrance door, and there were bells on the confessionals so that at any other time of the day one could ring a bell and a priest would appear.

Gradually her spiritual life deepened. A priest taught her to say the Little Office of the Blessed Virgin. She began to go to daily Communion and attended Benediction. She lived her life liturgically.

> Ritual, how could we do without it! Though it may seem to be gibberish and irreverence, though the Mass is offered up in such haste that the sacred sentence *hoc est corpus meum* was abbreviated into "hocus-pocus" by the bitter protestor and has come down into our language meaning trickery, nevertheless there is a sureness and a conviction there. And just as a husband may embrace his wife casually as he leaves for work in the morning, and kiss her absent-mindedly in his comings and goings, still that kiss on occasion turns to rapture, a burning fire of tenderness and love. And with this to stay her she demands the "ritual" of affection shown. The little altar boy kissing the cruet of water as he hands it to the priest is performing a rite. We have too little ritual in our lives.

Taken in conjunction with Peter Maurin's belief in "the gentle personalism of traditional Catholicism," what all this suggests is that the supposed conflict between a hierarchical Catholic Church and a non-hierarchical Christian anarchism simply didn't exist for the movement's founders. Dorothy Day was quick to criticize the Church's ministers when they failed to live up to the Church's social teaching but she was also quick to point out that "the priests were the dispensers of the Sacraments, bringing Christ to men."

Some of this liturgical vision has survived into the twenty-first century in the London Catholic Worker house, but much has not. There was no sign of the Little Office of the Blessed Virgin Mary, no sign of Benediction or daily Mass. The community gathers for morning and evening prayer "pretty much every day," a bell rings for silent prayer at the start of each meal, and the church still functions as a place of prayer. However, with the Blessed Sacrament no longer reserved in the tabernacle, there was little to differentiate the building from the Protestant church it had once been. Though full of stuff, it felt sadly empty.

**What is to be done?**
So, what is to be done? as Vladimir Lenin once asked. By the time I left Giuseppe Conlon House, I wasn't sure I had an answer. When Fr Martin spoke about the importance of their work, he emphasized the role of faith. Part of his work, he said, was to help sustain activists' faith in the Church, to show them they still had a place. At the same time, he hoped that those outside the Church might see the deeper significance of their work: "I've never seen Christians being visibly Christian in activism before," a fellow activist once told him to his great delight.

I was impressed by Fr Martin. He lives his faith wholeheartedly, embracing poverty and the corporal works of mercy in ways that put me to shame. He has struggled through difficult times when the Catholic Worker Movement was struggling to establish itself in the UK and then through the ups and downs of its first two decades. But I was less sure of the theology that underpinned the movement's work. Fr Martin told me that he had been inspired by Liberation Theology, and it certainly felt as though I had stepped back into the 1970s at times during my visit. However, nothing was quite as simple as it seemed, for Fr Martin was also inspired by the Worker Priest Movement, whose heyday was in the 1940s. What's more, he was happy to allow Extinction Rebellion to use the building for their meetings, which seemed to move the community deeply into the twenty-first century. It was difficult to know quite what to make of it, a photograph of Emmeline Pankhurst, a leading suffragette, on one of the bookcases summing up my uncertainty. Of course, I thought to myself, when I arrived. That's exactly who they'd have a picture of. No surprise there. But there was a surprise. Later during my visit, I grabbed an opportunity to take a closer look. It wasn't Emmeline Pankhurst at all: it was St Thérèse of Lisieux.

As I left to catch the bus back to the station, one phrase stuck in my mind: "The Catholic Worker Movement works better in practice than in theory," Fr Martin told me. I wondered if he was right.

# 7

# The Transalpine Redemptorists

FOR SOME TIME, I had been wanting to immerse myself in the traditional Catholicism of which Peter Maurin wrote and on which Dorothy Day so clearly relied, so I decided to go on retreat. The only question was, where was I to go? The world Dorothy Day described in her autobiography is now long gone, so there weren't a great many options. Casting my net wider than I had done so far on my travels, I eventually came across what looked like the perfect retreat venue and so started to prepare for my longest journey yet.

In 1689, the Japanese poet and Buddhist monk Matsuo Bashō set off on a journey which he later recorded in perhaps his most famous book, *The Narrow Way to the Deep North*. Bashō's aim was nothing less than to attain spiritual enlightenment by casting off the burdens of the material world. There is a world of difference between Buddhism and Christianity, but I couldn't help but think about Bashō's travels when, over three centuries later, I set off on my own narrow way to the deep north, though my destination was not Ōgaki but Papa Stronsay in Orkney, home of the Transalpine Redemptorists.

Before this trip to an island off the north coast of Scotland, my most extravagant journey in search of radical Christianity had been to Dover, but getting there had been a breeze in comparison. I'd simply jumped in my car and driven down to the south coast. Getting to Papa Stronsay was a different matter altogether. I planned extensively, writing different options in my notebook, matching plane, train, and ferry timetables, calculating times and connections with the precision of an advanced mathematical modeler. Eventually, I broke the journey down into nine distinct stages:

Stage 1: Catch a lift to our local station
Stage 2: Local train into London
Stage 3: Underground train across London
Stage 4: Caledonian Sleeper train from London to Edinburgh
Stage 5: Tram across Edinburgh to the airport
Stage 6: Plane from Edinburgh to Kirkwall in Orkney
Stage 7: Bus from Kirkwall Airport to Kirkwall Ferry Port
Stage 8: Ferry from Kirkwall to the island of Stronsay, twenty miles northeast of Kirkwall
Stage 9: A six-minute journey in the monks' boat across the bay to Papa Stronsay

It worked like a dream, the only issue being when part of the tram's inner casing fell on a fellow traveler's head just outside Edinburgh Airport. That incident aside, I was able to sit back and enjoy the pressures of the quotidian world dropping away as I steeped myself in silence. My retreat began the moment I stepped onto the train at my local station.

The Transalpine Redemptorists trace their foundation to St Alphonsus Liguori, whose own discernment to religious life can be dated to 1723. The Redemptorist order, which he founded in Scala, near Naples, soon spread outside Italy—it became transalpine—reaching every part of the globe by the twentieth century. One important development was the mission to Ukraine, led by the heroic bishop Charnetsky, who was imprisoned by the Soviets for many years before dying in 1959 as a result of his suffering in the camps. The Papa Stronsay monks' tiny boat is named for him.

However, the founding of Golgotha Monastery on Papa Stronsay can be dated more immediately to the time of the liturgical battles of the 1960s, '70s, and '80s. What marked those days above all was theological, pastoral, and liturgical confusion. Mired in the confusion of the time, a young Redemptorist priest from New Zealand tried to find a sure path on which to walk. With some encouragement from within his order (and some resistance too), Fr Michael Mary Sim set out for Écône in Switzerland, where Archbishop Lefe-

## The Transalpine Redemptorists

bvre had established the headquarters of the Society of St Pius X, whose raison d'être included the preservation of the Old Mass. In Switzerland, Fr Sim became convinced that "the crisis in the Church came from and was caused by a crisis in the Liturgy," as the Transalpine Redemptorists' website explains. What's more, he came to believe that he could remain faithful to the Old Mass *and* remain a Redemptorist, though his superiors in the order failed to see eye to eye with him on that matter. As a consequence, Fr Sim ended up founding a new monastery in a new country. With just a handful of companions, he moved to the Isle of Sheppey in England in 1988, building a new foundation on land given by a sympathetic benefactor. There the monastery became established and grew over the next decade. No longer in communion with Rome, it was regarded by some within the Church as utterly beyond the pale, though to others it seemed truly radical, preserving what much of the rest of the Church had so meekly surrendered in the years after the Second Vatican Council.

Then, in 1999, a new page was turned. The community bought the island of Papa Stronsay, formerly called Papey Minni, or "Little Priests' Island," after the monks of St Columba. The monks of Papa Stronsay were also mentioned in the great *Orkneyinga Saga*, though the island lost its monks at some point after the Viking era, so the return of a monastic community at the end of the second millennium was an exciting development in the island's history. The arrival of a new pope shortly afterwards brought yet more change. The election of Joseph Ratzinger as Pope Benedict XVI in 2005 was, in some ways, a vote for continuity. Ratzinger had been Pope John Paul II's right-hand man for many years. They shared the same mind on many matters and worked for the same priorities. However, Pope Benedict's attitude towards the liturgy was markedly different to that of his predecessor. John Paul II's great gifts to the Church were his encyclicals. He was a great teaching pope. Pope Benedict's encyclicals were also great gifts but he saw what, arguably, John Paul II could not: that the loss of the Old Mass was a loss to the whole Church. What's more, he was determined to do something about it. His motu proprio *Summorum Pontificum* offered relief for beleaguered Catholics who had clung to the Old Mass for decades and an opportunity for a new generation of Catholics to experience and fall in love with the Mass their forefathers had known and loved.

The reconciliation of the Society of St Pius X, for which Pope Benedict longed, did not take place, but the Transalpine Redemptorists at Papa Stronsay did take the olive branch which he offered across many seas. It took time and many negotiations before any decisions were finalized, but eventually the Transalpine Redemptorists were received back into full communion with the Church, retaining the traditional charism they had fought so long to preserve.

**A journey to the far north**
My own journey to the island monastery was far less tumultuous. In the spirit of pilgrimage, I took only a small bag and slept in my chair rather than in one of the plush beds that were on offer in the Caledonian Sleeper from London to Edinburgh. When we arrived in Scotland's capital city at 5 am, I was, therefore, both tired and hungry. Going off in search of breakfast, I wandered along Princes Street, past the Scott Monument—the largest monument to a writer in the world—and around the Scottish National Gallery. The lure of Edinburgh Castle looming above me on King Arthur's Mount proving too strong, I also hacked uphill to the Royal Mile, hoping that there at least a café would be open.

It is a strange thing to arrive in a capital city when it is still shaking itself out of sleep. The only people out and about at that time of the morning were the delivery drivers. I had freedom to roam or remain as I chose, so taking advantage of the space and ignoring my rumbling stomach, I stopped and sketched the view from on high before descending to the station once more in search of that elusive cup of coffee. Refreshed and reinvigorated, I then set out on further explorations, eventually finding myself outside the Writers' Museum. Carved into the stones at my feet were the words of some of Scotland's greatest writers, including at least two Catholic converts: Muriel Spark and George Mackay Brown. It was George Mackay Brown, the greatest of Orkney's many fine writers, who most intrigued me. I had recently managed to track down his correspondence with Sr Margaret Tournour, a Sacred Heart nun and woodcarver, and had spent a very pleasant morning reading about Stromness, where Brown lived semi-monastically in a tiny house overlooking the harbor. Here was a writer who treasured the past, an author who saw the past in the present. Maybe his work offered a way into the fraught debate about the place of the traditional Latin Mass in the Church.

With the exception of short stints at Newbattle Abbey and Edinburgh University, GMB (as he was often known) lived in Stromness, a few miles from Kirkwall, all his life. His home was Orkney and his theme was Orkney too: its history, its natural history, and its people. At the very center of his life and work was the towering figure of St Magnus, who had been born into an aristocratic Oracadian family in the late eleventh century. Though destined to become Earl of Orkney during a violent age, he was a peace-loving man, distinguishing himself at the Battle of the Menai Straits by remaining on deck singing psalms while the Norwegians who had compelled him to go a-Viking fought savagely around him.

I have said that Magnus was destined to become Earl of Orkney but so too was his cousin Hakon. In the complex domestic politics of their day, it was deemed safest to have the two men rule Orkney jointly rather than allow civil war to break out when the old earl died. It was a compromise that suited no one. As the *Orkenyinga Saga* recalls, "When the kinsmen had been ruling the earldom for some time, it so happened, as it often does, that malicious tongues set out to destroy their friendship, and it was to Hakon that the more luckless men were drawn, for he was very envious of the popularity and splendor of his cousin Magnus." In Easter 1115 Magnus was lured to the holy island of Egilsay for peace negotiations with a promise that Hakon would bring only two ships of unarmed men with him. Hakon did not keep that promise. Arriving with eight ships of fully armed men, he was determined to seize sole control of the islands, which meant dealing with Magnus once and for all. On Easter Monday, he ordered his cook to murder Magnus in cold blood, no one else being prepared to do the dishonorable deed.

George Mackay Brown's greatest novel, *Magnus*, retells the story of Magnus's martyrdom. Acutely aware that he was writing in and for a secular age, GMB took a radical approach to the story of Orkney's greatest saint, drawing strongly on the style and content of the *Orkneyinga Saga* and playing around with notions of time, silence, and sacrifice in his narrative. Remarkably for a work of fiction published by a mainstream publisher in the late twentieth century, it has the Eucharist at its center. Why did Brown build his narrative around the sacrifice of St Magnus and the sacrifice of the Mass? The answer probably lies in the context in which the book was written. GMB wrote *Magnus* in the early 1970s, when the sacrificial nature of the Mass was being questioned within the Catholic Church as well as from outside. He was writing at a time of great liturgical change, his novel being published shortly after the promulgation of Pope Paul VI's revised missal in 1969 and its first publication in 1970. With these disorienting events looming in the background, Brown began to struggle. As he later wrote in his autobiography, he had to acknowledge that "the whole story would strike a modern reader as remote and unconnected with our situation in the twentieth century." But rather than tone down St Magnus's miracles or sweep questions of sacrifice under the carpet, he took the bold decision to place the whole notion of sacrifice at the center of his novel. And that meant writing about the Mass.

According to the novel's narrator, the Mass is the "end and the beginning. All time was gathered up into that ritual half-hour, the entire history of mankind, as well the events that have not yet happened as the things recorded in chronicles and sagas." The events of the Mass cut across time and space, changing the individual from within, raising him to a new dignity, giving his words, actions, and thoughts a completely new significance: "Since all the round of time is gathered into this ritual half-hour, the actions of Everyman, once the bread of divine wisdom is in his body, have an immense importance; what he does and says and thinks reverberates through the whole web of time." It's quite a claim, especially in a novel written in and for a secular age. However, Brown doesn't shy away from it. Speaking about the death of Christ on the cross, his narrator tells us that this "was the one central sacrifice of history. *I am the bread of life.* All previous rituals had been a foreshadowing of this; all subsequent rituals a re-enactment. The fires at the centre of the earth, the sun above, all divine essences and ecstasies, come to this silence at last—a circle of bread and a cup of wine on an altar."

What we find in *Magnus*, in other words, is a profoundly radical vision of the power of sacrifice, not an antiquarian interest in liturgiology or a rose-tinted view of Catholic life in the years before the Second Vatican Council. Could the same be said of the Transalpine Redemptorists, I wondered? Leaving Edinburgh, I flew to Kirkwall, determined to find out.

## All at sea

It was clear that we had crossed some sort of boundary the moment we touched down at Kirkwall's tiny airport. The summer heat of Edinburgh had given way to a biting wind, but the noise and bustle of the city had also been replaced by a palpable sense of tranquility. The arrival and departure lounge was the size of a large high street café and there couldn't have been more than a few dozen people in the whole airport. As I waited for a bus to take me into town, I got to chatting with another visitor. Her husband was the Stronsay general practitioner for three months of the year and she was flying in to see him for the weekend. One doctor for three hundred people: the inhabitants of Stronsay may have the best GP service in the whole of the United Kingdom.

The bus took us through the countryside to Orkney's capital city (population: 10,000) where I had an hour or so before the ferry to Stronsay departed. Inspired by George Mackay Brown, I went straight to St Magnus Cathedral. Built in 1137 by St Rognvald, St Magnus's nephew, the cathedral is a magnificent red sandstone building, its blood-red stone a constant reminder of the martyr to whom it was dedicated and whose relics were found in a pillar in the sanctuary when the cathedral was restored in 1919. Almost certainly they had been placed there for protection when John Knox's reformers tore through the country in the mid-sixteenth century. I recalled George Mackay Brown's very first collection of poetry, in which he gave voice to Orkney as it once was and as it still could be:

> For the islands I sing
> and for a few friends;

not to foster means
or to be midwife to ends.

Not for old Marx
and his moon-cold logic—
anthill dialectics,
neither gay nor tragic.

Not that extravagance
Lawrence understood—
golden phoenix
flowering from blood.

For Scotland I sing,
the Knox-ruined nation,
that poet and saint
must rebuild with their passion.

As two fiddlers rehearsed for a concert, I paid my own homage to St Magnus, laying my hands on the pillar and asking for his prayers. But I couldn't stay for long, as I had that ferry to catch, a ferry which would take me out of Kirkwall, past Egilsay, the site of St Magnus's martyrdom, to Stronsay, where I hoped one of the Transalpine Redemptorist brothers would meet me.

I had come for Pentecost and so it seemed entirely appropriate that the wind swept over and around me as I walked along Kirkwall pier and onto the M.V. Varagen, redoubling its efforts the moment we pulled out of Kirkwall harbor. I stood on deck and braced myself against it, watching the sea birds—common terns, cormorants, and the occasional puffin—twisting low above the waves, elegant and strong. It looked as though they must be swamped, so powerful was the wind, so unpredictable the waves, but they never were. Like Gerard Manley Hopkins's windhover, they rode "the rolling level underneath [them] steady air." Could I too allow the Holy Spirit to blow me where he willed, I wondered, or would I try to hold my ground and be buffeted? I didn't know, but the closer I got to my destination the more I cloaked myself in prayer and hoped I would find what I was looking for.

# The Transalpine Redemptorists

We sailed through Stronsay Firth and out into Sanday Sound, passing several islands as we went: Shapinsay, Gairsay, Eday, and Sanday, as well as the much smaller Muckle Green Holm and Holm of Huip. Walking round the deck, I caught a glimpse of Egilsay in the distance. Then, finally, we arrived, sailing between Stronsay and Papa Stronsay into the harbor at Whitehall, once a thriving fishing community, now a few houses on the seafront. After a long, long journey, I was almost at my destination.

But not quite. Though I could clearly see Papa Stronsay across the water—could almost throw a pebble from one shore to the next—we couldn't get there. That was the message the monk who met me gave. The wind was too strong. There was no way we'd be able to moor up. After all that time and planning, I had to be content with a night in a small guest house by the chapel at the end of the pier and night prayers in the chapel itself with a couple of the monks who were temporarily away from the monastery. However, as it was now the Vigil of Pentecost, the rule of silence for my two new friends was relaxed, so over a leisurely but extremely basic meal of baked beans and bread, we had a long chat about the monastery and how we'd each ended up—or, in my case, almost ended up—there. It wasn't quite working out as the silent retreat I'd planned, but it turned out to be a great evening.

Like several other monks I've met before, the priest who welcomed me was a convert from evangelical Protestantism. A former Presbyterian who'd wanted to become a Protestant missionary, he had the courage to follow the truth wherever it took him, which was to a Catholic college (where he converted), to a FSSP parish (where he became a traditionalist), and, at the age of twenty-four, into the monastery. Now in his thirties, he is one of the older members of the community. This was what struck me most forcibly the next day when the rest of the monks sailed over in their small boat from the monastery to the chapel on Stronsay for sung Mass: the average age of the community. The youngest of the monks had recently celebrated his twenty-first birthday and the majority of the others were in their twenties. At a time when many monastic communities are slowly dying out, here was one that was not simply surviving but flourishing.

*Travels in Radical Christianity*

But why? What is it about the Transalpine Redemptorists that makes their order so attractive to young men from around the world? The answer seemed clear. At the heart of the community is a devotion to the liturgy, to the public prayer of the Church as it has been done for hundreds of years. On a typical day the monks rise at 4:55 and are in the chapel half an hour later for private prayer, meditation, Matins, Lauds, and Mass. Breakfast comes three or so hours after rising. And so the day continues. The Angelus at noon, a decade of the Dolors of Our Lady at 2.30, rosary at 5:30, night prayers at 7:30, lights out and the Great Silence at 9 pm. As St Benedict wrote, many hundreds of years before, "nothing is to be preferred to the Work of God." In the 21st century, this total devotion to God through prayer seems inexplicable to many people. In its own way it is just as radical as the activism of the Catholic Worker Movement. Maybe more so because it is so counter-cultural. Therein lies its strength. I was reminded of a beautiful passage in Evelyn Waugh's diaries (repeated almost word for word in a letter to the *Catholic Herald*) in which he explains his reasons for converting:

> When I first came into the Church I was drawn not by splendid ceremonies but by the spectacle of the priest as a craftsman. He had an important job to do which none but he was qualified for. He and his apprentice stumped up to the altar with their tools and set to work without a glance to those behind them, still less with any intention to make a personal impression on them.

Here too on Papa Stronsay there were craftsmen at work. The liturgy on Papa Stronsay was beautiful in the way a hand-crafted cabinet is beautiful. It wasn't showy or self-consciously antiquated. It simply was what it was always meant to be: prayer, a work of God, a sign of what is to come. If this is radical then it is a radicalism that is rooted in the essential mysteries of the faith.

An effect of the liturgy, and a precondition for it, is silence. Catching the ferry back to Kirkwall from Stronsay after my retreat, it was a shock to hear tinny voices emerging from a cell phone once again. On Papa Stronsay there were no TVs, no radios, no computers that I ever saw. But there was more to the silence of the island than an absence of electronic noise. What the monks sought was a

## The Transalpine Redemptorists

listening silence, a silence from distractions which makes it easier to listen to God in the depths of our hearts. On the island I became acutely aware that God is so close and yet so difficult to hear because we become so adept at shutting Him out. As Blessed Marie-Eugène de l'Enfant-Jésus put it in *I Want to See God*, the book I brought with me for my spiritual reading,

> We live in a fever of movement and activity. Evil isn't found only in the organization of modern life, in the haste which it imposes on our gestures, the speed and ease of travel which it allows. A deeper evil is found in the feverish nervousness of our temperaments. We don't know how to wait any more nor how to be silent. And yet we seem to be searching for silence and solitude. We leave familiar places to search for new horizons, for another atmosphere, but as often as not it's only so we can entertain ourselves with new impressions. And yet, however much times change, God stays the same, *Tu autem idem Ipse es*. He always speaks his Word in silence and it is in silence that the soul must receive it.

Silence and solitude. These are the attractions of Papa Stronsay. Silence in which to listen to God and solitude to preserve and enable that silence. As Blessed Marie-Eugène explained later in *I Want to See God*, silence isolates us from the external world, allowing, or even obliging, us to enter into the interior world we have been seeking.

And yet on that first Sunday, after the glories of sung Mass, I found the silence and solitude of my cell terrifying. Suddenly, after hours of travel and a term immersed in the busyness of school and the noise of home, I was alone and isolated. That was how it felt. I was stuck in my cell with only myself for company and it was suddenly too much. (It didn't help that the monks had left a stone skull, a *memento mori*, on my desk. I stuck it on a shelf, facing the wall.) I had to get out. I couldn't stay there any longer. Slipping out of the door, I clambered up a grassy bank—no doubt surprising the pilgrim in the cell next door—and looked for some sort of relief in the natural beauty of the island. Climbing a gate, I set off down a path past the hundred or so sheep the monks farm, looking for a different kind of silence and solitude. Silence and solitude that didn't oblige me to confront myself. I was missing my family desperately, but it wasn't human company I needed at that moment. It was the musical silence of the natural world.

As I hiked towards the shore, an escort of oystercatchers tracked my every step, piping their shrill alarm as I wandered through their territory. The gulls roosting on the shoreline seemed less alarmed. Unless I wandered very close, not noticing their presence, they didn't move. I was finding the monastic experience mentally and spiritually agitating: they were a model of calm contemplation.

I kept going, listening to the wind and the cries of wheeling birds—cormorants, terns, distant geese—and stopping every now and again to look at one of the delicate coastal flowers that thrived in that hostile environment: wild angelica with its spiky leaves; thrift growing between cracks in the great slabs of sedimentary rocks that sat above the beach; Scots lovage clustering along the coastal path, or what I imagined could be a path if I walked it with enough determination. And then, as I rounded the final headland, I saw what I'd been hoping to see all along: A solitary seal popped his head out of the sea and swam slowly up the coastline.

**No worries**

Was this the fourth reason, after the liturgy, silence, and solitude, that young men are attracted to the monastic life on Papa Stronsay? I asked myself. Is it the natural beauty of Orkney that calls men halfway round the world? (For nearly half the monks came from New Zealand. "No worries," they said when I thanked them for the meals they brought to my cell.) I think not. The Transalpine Redemptorists now have a foundation in Montana, which is a beautiful place in its own way, but it isn't the beauty of the countryside that beckons, it's the desert. No longer the arid wastes of Egypt as it was for the first Christian monks, but a place far from what are usually regarded as the centers of civilization. The suspicion—maybe the accusation—must be that these young men are *fleeing* the world, that becoming a monk is an unhealthy form of escapism.

That is the argument, but it's an argument that simply doesn't work. The monks I met were all devastatingly normal. They wouldn't

## The Transalpine Redemptorists

have been out of place in any place where young people usually gather. They were clearly at ease with themselves. They weren't running away because they couldn't cope. What's more, it soon became apparent that, despite its location, the monastery wasn't actually cut off from the world in any meaningful sense. Some of the monks travel great distances to offer Mass, while the brothers routinely travel long distances too, going wherever they are asked to run retreats and other activities. Their escape, if escape it is, is of quite a different order. What distinguishes these monks—what makes them radical—is their decision to live in a desert in the middle of the pathless seas so they can secure their own salvation with fear and trembling. Then, strengthened by their tactical withdrawal, they attack in strength, first and foremost through their prayers, as contemplatives have always done. This is not to say that the beauty of Papa Stronsay is unimportant, but it is to draw attention to the true nature of the monks' vocation and of their radicalism.

Back in my cell, I began to adjust to the structure of the monks' day, to the rhythm of the Divine Office. At the heart of monasticism is an elevated understanding of time. Just like George Mackay Brown, the Transalpine Redemptorists believe that time is not empty but liturgical. Past, present, and future are caught up in the mystery of the crucifixion, which is daily re-presented on the altars of their chapels. What this means in solidly practical terms is that the day is punctuated by liturgical prayer and by the ringing of the monastery's great bells. After the shock of the opening day's silence and solitude, I began to settle into this new way of structuring my day, wondering whether I could take this monastic approach to time into the world outside the monastery. It is true that there are lay people who pray the monastic hours in the midst of their busy lives, but it's difficult to see how this could be possible for most families. Solitude and silence are in short supply when young children enter the picture. Maybe that's why Dorothy Day turned to the Little Office of the Blessed Virgin Mary, a form of the Divine Office adapted specifically for laypeople hundreds of years ago. This Little Office can be prayed by those who are still in the world, not without difficulty but with comparative ease since its use eventually becomes habitual.

*Travels in Radical Christianity*

However, there is another way of considering the question, and that is to consider the very notion of structuring the day. We all structure our day, whether we are monks or laypeople. The only difference is the way we structure it. Some of us structure our day with cups of tea or coffee. Or maybe we turn to the radio or TV for regular news updates. Perhaps we check our phones and computers for messages. There are many ways of breaking up those twenty-four long hours. In my cell, all those options were removed. I couldn't have a cup of tea whenever I wanted. I couldn't reach for the snack cupboard, switch on the radio, or check emails. I was thrown back onto whatever was left when all those props were removed. That is why I was scared of the solitude and silence at first. In daily life, I regularly voiced a desire for more time, more silence, fewer work obligations. Now that I had my wish, I struggled with my newfound freedom. What I had to learn in the monastery was how to structure my day with prayer. What I had to take back home with me were my newfound habits. Only time would tell how successful I might be.

On my final morning in the monastery, I woke up half an hour before the monastery bell sounded: at 4:20. At five o'clock I got up, packed my few belongings, and made my way to the chapel to join the monks for Matins and Lauds. Then I walked to the pier, where the boat was ready to take me across to Stronsay and the waiting ferry. I was on my way home.

# 8

# Home Education

MY JOURNEY HOME was more straightforward than the journey up had been. I took the ferry from Stronsay to Kirkwall, caught the bus to the airport, and then flew into Aberdeen for a connecting flight to Heathrow. From there I could take a train into central London and then another train home. What I hadn't realized, being away on my tech-free, silent retreat, was that a train strike had been announced. When I arrived late in the evening at London's Victoria Station, I found a locked gate. The station was closed and I had no obvious way of getting home.

Two night buses and a very expensive taxi later, I stumbled through my front door at 2 am, aching for bed. As I sank down onto my pillow, I gave thanks for my retreat and settled down for a good, long sleep. Half an hour later, my youngest daughter called me from her bed and was promptly sick all over the duvet.

Over the next few days we all went down with the vomiting bug and I quickly forgot about the peace and silence of Orkney. This is a picture that any parent will recognize. We may have all sorts of beautiful plans for a well-lived life, but reality soon kicks in when children arrive on the scene. "Take from our lives the strain and stress / And let our ordered lives confess / The beauty of Thy peace," the hymn says, but it's a hymn that couldn't have been written by any parent of young kids. So, what might radical Christianity look like for families? That was a question which haunted me throughout my travels. I'd met families who lived in the Bruderhof community, and families who have drawn great encouragement from the Manquehue Apostolic Movement and Opus Dei. But was there a more radical approach still? Was there a way of being radically Christian in a world that is messy and often confusing? I believed there was, because we were already beginning to live it ourselves as home educators.

There are some journeys whose first steps we never expect, and there are others which take us where we never thought to go. Sometimes those journeys are one and the same: the ones with unexpected beginnings, uncertain wanderings, and unknown ends. Sometimes they are the ones which bring us the greatest joy. So it was with us. We had no plans to home-educate our children, and when we started we were not committed to it for any longer than a year. But as I write, almost ten years on from those curious first steps, we find ourselves still on the road.

So far so poetic. What did all this mean in practice? To answer that question, I need to step back for a moment and consider my own schooling. My own experience of education was entirely conventional. That is, conventional as most people in the UK understand it. I went to my local primary school, local secondary school, and then university. Even though I studied history at university, I had no idea that what most people regard as the educational norm—compulsory schooling, whole-class teaching, and fixed-length university degrees—is a comparatively recent innovation. Neil Postman, who was a particularly powerful myth-puncturer, points out in *Technopoly* that even "the seemingly harmless practice of assigning marks or grades to the answers students give" is a modern anomaly, invented by William Farish, an obscure Cambridge tutor, in 1792:

> To say that someone should be doing better work because he has an IQ of 134, or that someone is a 7.2 on a sensitivity scale, or that this man's essay on the rise of capitalism is an A- and that this man's is a C+, would have sounded like gibberish to Galileo or Shakespeare or Thomas Jefferson.

My understanding of all this came later, after we started home-educating. Until that time, I was happily ignorant. I'd been to school. Everyone I knew had been to school. I'd gone to university. Most of my peers went to university. I'd chosen a career because what other option did I have? Then we adopted our first child and everything changed.

## Home Education

After our daughter had spent a couple years at a local Catholic school, we started to consider other options. Now that we knew that parents are the primary educators of their children, we did what parents do best: we listened to the unspoken messages our daughter was sending us. Messages she didn't necessarily know she was sending herself because she was only six years old. The details of those days are, in a sense, unimportant. What mattered for our daughter might not be what matters for yours. Her story is hers alone (though something similar to it is, we discovered, familiar to many families.) But the net result was that one day my wife suggested we consider home education. I was skeptical.

In the UK, home education is still a radical option. In fact, as far as I was concerned, it wasn't even an option. The only homeschooled student I'd ever set eyes on was a mathematical prodigy who became something of a minor celebrity when she graduated from Oxford University at the age of thirteen. I occasionally saw her cycling around the city on the back of the tandem steered by her father. She must have been 15 or 16 years old at the time and she was studying for her DPhil (as a PhD is called in Oxford). My youthful, conventional self recoiled from this unusual way of doing things. I shoved home education to the back of my mind and forgot all about it.

After Oxford, when I was working in the night shelter for homeless men in Leeds, my prejudices against home education were confirmed. The evening shifts in the shelter were hard because they were liable to turn violent, but the night shifts were difficult in another way. Adjusting to an entirely different circadian rhythm was beyond my natural powers, so I turned to late-night TV in an attempt to keep myself awake. Sitting in our bleak office, I watched some bizarre discussion programmes in the middle of the night, none of which made any lasting impression on me. None, that is, bar one. That particular episode featured a home-educated, bow-tie-wearing child, as precocious in his own way as the tandem-riding mathematician, though perhaps more self-confident. From that moment onwards, my mind was made up. Home education was to be avoided at all costs.

*Travels in Radical Christianity*

**Star of the Week**

So when, twenty years later, my wife suggested we consider home-schooling, I had nothing to fall back on but my own experience of education and a few distant, and faintly troubling, memories to guide me. Fortunately, my wife did her homework, dragging me along with her. We read books and blogs. We chatted to people who had been home-educating for years. We started to make plans. Slowly, I began to discover that there is a great deal more to home education than hothouse parenting and bow-ties. I began to sense that home education is simply a natural extension of the parental roles we already had. As soon as we decided to take the plunge, I started planning math lessons while my wife asked our daughter what she'd like to study.

"Greek," she replied.

"OK!" we said, with scarcely a moment's hesitation. "We'll see what we can arrange."

"And please can we have assemblies?" she added.

That was a little harder to arrange. After all, at that stage our home school had a grand total of one student. Nonetheless, we did our best. On that first Monday of the school year—because it hadn't yet occurred to us that school years are another arbitrary convention we don't have to follow—we launched our home education battle plan. We had an elaborate timetable, an organized bookshelf, and a few worried relatives: "Don't worry. We can always put her back in school if it doesn't work," we told them, happy to have this backup option ourselves.

That first week was fun. We started Greek (with Minimus the Mouse), we played educational CDs on car journeys, and we stuck to the timetable, which meant that when Friday arrived we had our first assembly. To no one's surprise but our daughter's, she was Star of the Week, receiving a big sticker as her reward. Everyone was happy.

It couldn't, and didn't, last. We ran out of Greek lessons. The CDs didn't all hold our daughter's attention. The timetable—assemblies and all—slowly fell apart. But we didn't give up: we relaxed. And, as we relaxed, we listened to the wisdom of the home-educating families we were now meeting every week.

## Home Education

One of the great surprises about home education was that you can do it without ever being at home. While I went to work, my wife seemed to spend her life on the road. Our daughter joined a home educators' art class and a home educators' gymnastics group. My wife drove down the motorway for a Catechesis of the Good Shepherd atrium. She organized an impressive program of educational visits, traveling into London for concerts, museum trips, and social gatherings. Between us, we packed the week with events and activities and wondered why we were fraying at the edges.

However, we also gradually learned that there is a world of difference between homeschooling and home education. To quote Neil Postman again, "education is not the same thing as schooling, and ... in fact, not much of our education takes place in school." We discovered that we didn't need to mimic school, nor did we need to prove to our friends, relatives, and even ourselves that our daughter would be more successful at home than at school. We started to ask what education really means.

It amazes me now that I never asked that basic question before. As an experienced schoolteacher, I simply got on with preparing my students for the next set of exams. I mastered the content of whatever syllabus I was given, I managed my classroom, and I measured my results. Mastery, management, and measurement: that is what my teaching had become. Now all of a sudden, I was meeting people who thought differently, people who asked simple but profound questions about the fundamental aim of education.

### It's all Greek to me

My daughter's Greek lessons didn't last very long, but I'd studied Greek as a child and had enjoyed the language so much that I even booked myself into Greek summer schools during my teen years, but I'd never connected what I read in those lessons with life in the modern world. I'd never seriously considered the notion that Socrates, Plato, or Aristotle might have something to teach us in the twenty-first century. I'd certainly never heard anyone recommend a classical education.

All that has now changed. Thinking about the true purpose of education changed the way we approached home education, but, unexpectedly, it also changed my attitude towards school-teaching. A few years ago, I was given the opportunity to create a new course for my school's sixth-form students. After some consideration, we decided to call it the Sophia program because *sophia* is the Greek word for wisdom. I started by asking my students some questions:

> What is the point of education?
>
> The ancient Greeks would have phrased the question differently. They would have asked, what is the end of education? What is its *telos*? Where is it heading? Phrased like that, the question becomes positive, even inspiring.
>
> And they would have asked it in the context of a broader question: what is the end of human existence?
>
> The simple answer to that complicated question, Aristotle said, was happiness or human flourishing. For humans to be happy and flourish, we need the best that education can give us: not qualifications but wisdom. Or, to give it its Greek name, *sophia*.

But who is Sophia? What is wisdom?

> We need a whole lifetime to answer that question, so for the time being we will limit ourselves to saying that wisdom is an understanding of the whole of reality. Modern education tends to fragment knowledge into separate subjects, separate lessons, and separate pieces of information which are learned for exams and then forgotten. But that's not how it should be.
>
> Our aim in the Sophia Program is to put things together again, to develop an understanding of the whole of reality. That is why our central image is a Subway Map of knowledge. It's the connections that matter.

Students can find these questions and this ancient wisdom unsettling, but they also find them strangely liberating. No longer are they being asked to jump through examination hoops. They are being given the opportunity to think, to consider what truly matters, and to work together in the pursuit of the wisdom that should be the true end of education, its *telos*. That's why I asked them to look at this beautiful passage from the Wisdom of Solomon (6:12–16) before we began our seminars in school:

# Home Education

> Wisdom is radiant and unfading,
> and she is easily discerned by those who love her,
> and is found by those who seek her.
> She hastens to make herself known to those who desire her.
> He who rises early to seek her will have no difficulty,
> for he will find her sitting at his gates.
> To fix one's thought on her is perfect understanding,
> and he who is vigilant on her account will soon be free from care,
> because she goes about seeking those worthy of her,
> and she graciously appears to them in them in their paths,
> and meets them in every thought.

Asking questions about the nature and purpose of education also liberated us as parents. We thought about what we really wanted for our daughter and adapted our approach accordingly. We stopped homeschooling and started home-educating. We stopped replicating what we had experienced in schools ourselves and started to make use of the freedom that being at home gave. When our main educational aim became wisdom rather than exam certificates, what we did at home changed too. When I realized that wisdom is the true end of education, I began to teach at school in a different way too.

**Singing math**

We knew now that the education we offered our daughter could look radically different from the education we had ourselves received, but we still weren't sure of the details. Then, one day, my wife told me she'd met a family who were part of a local homeschool group we hadn't yet visited. "They sing a lot," she said.

I can't remember what I replied but I probably put the conversation from my mind, thinking that joining a choir would be another great activity for my daughter. However, joining a choir wasn't on the agenda. The mission of Classical Conversations, a US program which is now catching on in the UK, is "to know God and make Him known." Everything else flows from that basic aim:

- God trusts parents with their children, and so should we.
- Wrestling with truth promotes blessing and virtue for the whole community.

- Education is the responsibility of the family, with support from fellow believers.
- The support of community enhances our ability to fulfill parental duties.
- The accountability of community both sharpens and humbles its members.
- Classical education embodies the most natural tools of learning.
- Truth is required to inculcate wisdom, knowledge, and understanding.
- Classical education prepares us to accept the responsibilities of Christian freedom.

The three fundamentals of Classical Conversations (CC) are Christianity, a classical model of education, and community. Each week, home-educating families gather for a community day, where they learn together, following a classical program that is designed to counteract the modern tendency towards fragmentation in education. But that's not what my children told me when they visited for the first time. They told me that they sang math. (Actually, that's not what they said, because we're British. They said, "We sang maths." As I raised a British eyebrow, they added, "And history and science and geography and Latin and…" "Stop, stop!" I interrupted. "You'd better explain." And so I should too.)

What I found when I eventually got to visit was a vibrant community of Christian families from various backgrounds. Classical Conversations itself has an evangelical foundation, but we also met Catholic and Orthodox families at the community day. What each of these families shared was a firm belief that parents are the primary educators of their children, that we work best when we work together, and that God has to be at the center of any meaningful education. The centrality of God is emphasized in a strikingly visual way in the classrooms of the younger groups, each parent-teacher working with a whiteboard on which is written the memory work for that week—math, history, science, geography, Latin and so on—spiraling out from "God," which takes center position on the board.

The Latin took me by surprise (even though we'd tried Greek lessons with my daughter at home). Latin for 5-year-olds? Really? And the science wasn't exactly straightforward either. Newton's first law of motion for toddlers? It seemed a big ask. But then the lesson started and everything started to fall into place. My children had been right. They really did sing everything: a timeline of history, Latin declensions, and Newtonian definitions included. The tunes were catchy, the children were enthusiastic, and the results were tangible. The children really knew their stuff.

The families I met were amazing, and I liked what I saw of the work the children were doing, but I was still somewhat baffled. This wasn't education as I had experienced it, nor was it homeschooling as we were doing it. These families had a different educational toolkit from the one we were using and I wanted to find out more.

## The lost tools of learning

In search of this lost educational toolkit, I eventually found my way to Dorothy L. Sayers's "The Lost Tools of Learning." This essay, which has been hugely influential in the USA if not so much in the UK where it originated, began life as a paper read at a vacation course in education at Oxford in 1947. It is a brilliant meditation on education, being both wise and funny, which is not a combination you tend to find in educational vision statements.

At the start of her talk, Sayers identified a problem: "The great defect of our education today [is] that although we often succeed in teaching our pupils 'subjects,' we fail lamentably on the whole in teaching them how to think." In some ways, it's a very modern complaint, though, of course, it has been voiced many times before. Here's John Henry Newman in *The Idea of a University*, for example, worrying about minds that "cannot fix their gaze on one object for two seconds together" and about students who "profess that they do not like logic, they do not like algebra, they have no taste for mathematics; which only means that they do not like application, they do not like attention, they shrink from the effort and labour of thinking, and the process of true intellectual gymnastics."

Newman's comments about attention are particularly interesting because they anticipate the thoughts of such later writers as Simone Weil and Matthew Crawford, both of whom pay a great deal of attention to the problem of inattention in our contemporary world.

But what's the solution? How can we "produce a society of educated people, fitted to preserve their intellectual freedom amid the complex pressures of our modern society," as Sayers puts it? Her answer is to "turn back the wheel of progress some four or five hundred years, to the point at which education began to lose sight of its true object." In this perception, she was wholly at one with Newman. They both believed in a traditional (which is to say, a classical) liberal education. Dorothy L. Sayers's great innovation, however, was to link each part of the Trivium—grammar, logic (or dialectic), and rhetoric—with a separate stage in children's development. She believed that children naturally pass through a Grammar stage before moving on to a Dialectic and then a Rhetoric stage. It is only when they have experienced the first three stages of development that they are truly equipped for the Quadrivium, the study of separate subjects in any meaningful sense. Sayers points out that grammar and dialectic

> are not what we should call "subjects" at all: they are only methods of dealing with subjects. Grammar, indeed, is a "subject" in the sense that it does mean definitely learning a language—at that period it meant learning Latin. But language itself is simply the medium in which thought is expressed. The whole of the Trivium was, in fact, intended to teach the pupil the proper use of the tools of learning, before he began to apply them to "subjects" at all. First, he learned a language; not just how to order a meal in a foreign language, but the structure of a language, and hence of language itself—what it was, how it was put together, and how it worked. Secondly, he learned how to use language; how to define his terms and make accurate statements; how to construct an argument and how to detect fallacies in argument. Dialectic, that is to say, embraced Logic and Disputation. Thirdly, he learned to express himself in language—how to say what he had to say elegantly and persuasively.

These tools of learning, Sayers believed, have been lost. We might still find a screwdriver lying around the house, or a chisel rusting in the corner of the garage, but we don't know how to use them effectively anymore: "Bits and pieces of the mediaeval tradition still linger, or have been revived, in the ordinary school syllabus of today... but these activities are cultivated more or less in detachment, as belonging to the special subjects in which they are pigeonholed rather than as forming one coherent scheme of mental training to which all 'subjects' stand in a subordinate relation." In her view, we stand on the other side of a great divide: "Modern education concentrates on 'teaching subjects,' leaving the method of thinking, arguing, and expressing one's conclusions to be picked up by the scholar as he goes along; mediaeval education concentrated on first forging and learning to handle the tools of learning, using whatever subject came handy as a piece of material on which to doodle until the use of the tool became second nature."

This, surely, is a very perceptive analysis not only of the educational landscape in Dorothy L. Sayers's day but in ours too. The great tradition lingers, but that is all. Whatever subject we teach—and that is still how most teachers think of themselves, as subject specialists—we hope our students will be able to write fluently, argue persuasively, and spot errors quickly, but we haven't really got time, or even the expertise, to teach these skills ourselves. We hope that someone else is onto it, and if they aren't, well, we've still got the syllabus to get through and the exams are rather pressing, so we concentrate on what's still under our control.

All of which brings us back to the singing of math. Many Christian classical home education programs are built on a version of Sayers's educational vision. They have a spiral curriculum so that students, beginning at the grammar stage, memorize lots of facts which they don't yet fully understand before they move on to the dialectic stage, when they begin to use this knowledge. Eventually they are able to move on to the rhetoric stage, where they focus more on ways of presenting their ideas clearly, beautifully, and truthfully.

That's why five-year-olds in Classical Conversations communities sing about the Treaty of Tordesillas, aquatic biomes, and the first-conjugation future tense. They may not be able to explain any of the facts they have learned, but when they move on to the dialectic stage they have them at their fingertips. Like tools. They can't make a cabinet but they know their way round a chisel. (For health and safety purposes, I would like to make it clear that I am, of course, writing entirely metaphorically.)

**New challenges**

I should make it clear, though, that there is a great deal more to Classical Conversations than singing. The younger children in Foundation groups also do science experiments and art, and give presentations each week. Then, after several cycles of learning, they move on to the Essentials stage, where they work at a much more advanced level. At this stage, parents start to discover one of the major joys of home education: that they are learning along with their children. Since most of us weren't classically educated, we soon discover that we all have major gaps in our knowledge and understanding. After the Essentials stage, students move on to the Challenge stage, studying a wide range of topics in seminar-style classes. To give just one example of what this means in practice, we could compare the list of books I teach my ninth-grade students in school with the ones ninth-grade students study in their Classical Conversations classes. In school we cover some modern poetry, some modern non-fiction extracts, Dickens's *A Christmas Carol*, Orwell's *Animal Farm*, and Shakespeare's *Macbeth*. In CC, students read *Everyman*, *Ben Hur*, *Sir Gawain and the Green Knight*, *Paradise Lost* (Book 1), *The Pilgrim's Progress*, *Up from Slavery*, Pushkin's *The Captain's Daughter*, *Jane Eyre*, *A Christmas Carol*, *Les Misérables*, *The Screwtape Letters*, and several other books. In school we talk a lot about the importance of stretch and challenge: in CC it's built into the curriculum.

It would be easy to focus on what Classical Conversations doesn't do—the children don't work on computers during community days, the parent-teachers don't talk about SMART targets or measurable outcomes—but that would be to miss the point. At the heart of this home education program is a practical vision rooted in an educational philosophy that only seems radical because it has been largely forgotten. It doesn't take long for any visitor to see that it works. The children learn lots, have lots of friends, and grow up to be faithful citizens. Given all this, it's hard to see why home education still causes suspicion in some quarters today.

Home Education

Prejudice is certainly part of the reason—I can say this because I used to have this prejudice myself—but home education also presents a challenge which demands a response. Here, for example, is Dorothy L. Sayers again, making a daring, perhaps even provocative, comment towards the end of her essay about the lost tools of learning:

> At the end of the Dialectic, the children will probably seem to be far behind their coevals brought up on old-fashioned "modern" methods, so far as detailed knowledge of specific subjects is concerned. But after the age of fourteen they should be able to overhaul the others hand over fist. Indeed, I am not at all sure that a pupil thoroughly proficient in the Trivium should not be fit to proceed immediately to the university at the age of sixteen, thus proving himself the equal of his medieval counterpart, whose precocity often appears to us so astonishing and unaccountable.

Is this a ridiculous argument? The evidence from home-educating families suggests that it is not, as I discovered when I set out on my travels once more, this time to Knock in Ireland.

### Heaven and Harvard

After home-educating for some years and writing about our experiences in a couple of books and several articles, I was excited to receive my first invitation to travel overseas to speak about the joys of home education. Would I give three talks at a home education conference in Knock, home of the great Irish Marian shrine? Of course, I would.

Compared with my journey to Orkney, getting to Knock was a breeze, not least because the village of Knock (population: 972) has its own international airport. The story of the building of the airport could fill a chapter in itself—in fact, it has already been turned into a musical—because it is so bizarre. The airport was the brainchild of the parish priest of Knock, Monsignor James Horan, who announced his plans on national TV in 1981, telling the interviewer, as diggers drove up and down the boggy terrain behind him, "We're building an airport and I hope the Department of Transport doesn't hear about it. Now don't tell them. . . . We've no money, but we're hoping to get it next week, or the week after." Five years later the airport was finished.

Home educators need that kind of faith. Stepping away from the supposed security of schools is a bold step, which is why I'd been invited to Ireland. With many families now considering home education, those of us who had already embarked on the journey were being asked to talk about our experiences.

Knock is a beautiful place. Like Walsingham, England's national Marian shrine, it is a peaceful village, but its basilica reminded me of Lourdes in scale and grandeur. The home education conference was on a different scale, a bunch of families gathered in one large meeting room. The discussions we had over the weekend were inspiring but it is the people I remember more. Some were home-educating already, while others were still considering their options. Among those who were already on the path, the majority were following the Catholic, classical curriculum offered by the Mother of Divine Grace School. The Mother of Divine Grace (popularly known as MODG) approach is very similar to the one offered by Classical Conversations, though MODG communities do not come together for weekly community days. Lessons take place either in the home or online under the supervision of a MODG consultant.

As with CC, "the classical method is fundamental to Mother of Divine Grace School. It permeates every aspect of our program from the selection and application of texts to our interactions with parents and students through our consultations and teacher programs." Though the language is Catholic rather than Protestant, its aims are also remarkably similar since it draws on many of the same sources: notably the work of Aristotle, Aquinas, and Dorothy L. Sayers:

> The end of education is wisdom. Man desires by nature to know, and that means we want to have not only the facts, but the reasons for the facts. We want to think about the highest things, the most noble, the most interesting in themselves. Liberal education, which we also call classical education, is such an education. It begins in wonder and aims at wisdom. It involves the seven liberal arts: grammar, logic, rhetoric, arithmetic, geometry, music, and astronomy. It also includes the study of nature, the

soul, ethics and politics, the highest created objects, and finally that to which all the others are ordered—theology, an understanding of the divine. Liberal education in its perfection is Catholic education, for it has the same end, identically, as the Catholic faith: the highest, best, and most perfect object, God.

It's a noble vision, but does it work? The answer I was given by a MODG graduate who joined us for a meal at the end of the conference was a resounding yes. Having gone through the entire program, she had been offered a place at medical school by four different British universities, the maximum number you can apply for. Of course, getting a place at medical school isn't necessarily a sign of wisdom, though the MODG graduate I chatted to seemed both wise and knowledgeable. Some home educators like to say that the purpose of education is heaven, not Harvard, though one home-educating friend insists that it should be both heaven *and* Harvard since there is no incompatibility between spiritual and academic excellence. With increasing numbers of students now graduating from Christian classical homeschool programs, evidence of the short-, medium-, and long-term success of this approach to education certainly seems to be growing. Here is a radical approach to Christian education which needn't scare the living daylights out of everyone.

**Awe and wonder**
One of the most striking features of the home education scene in the UK over the last few years has been the way families gravitate towards certain centers, often moving home and job in order to do so. There are now thriving home education communities in Walsingham, Preston, Reading, and Bedford, to name just a few. Many, but not all, of the families in these places follow a Christian classical homeschool program, but even within these groups of classical homeschoolers there is a great variety of approaches. Students attending the highly successful Regina Caeli Academy (RCA), for example, wear a uniform, which immediately sets the academy apart from most other homeschool groups, though the inspiration behind it is very similar to the vision which underpins Classical

*Travels in Radical Christianity*

Conversations and the Mother of Divine Grace School. One crucial difference is that children meet twice a week for lessons in the academy, studying at home for the rest of the week. It is a genuinely Catholic, classical community.

It's also a community which takes wonder seriously. As one of their publications explains, "the classical method is intended first and foremost to encourage the student's natural wonder and then give him the tools to pursue wonder throughout his life. Education is, in the Catholic vision, an atmosphere of wonder, a habit of virtue, and the joy of discovery." That is a beautiful and radical description of home education; if education is rooted in wonder then it should, and often does, look wholly unlike the school scene described (ironically) by Dorothy Sayers in "The Lost Tools of Learning":

> One has only to look at any school or examination syllabus to see that it is cluttered up with a great variety of exhausting subjects which [teachers] are called upon to teach, and the teaching of which sadly interferes with what every thoughtful mind will allow to be their proper duties, such as distributing milk, supervising meals, taking cloak-room duty, weighing and measuring pupils, keeping their eyes open for incipient mumps, measles and chicken-pox, making out lists, escorting parties round the Victoria and Albert Museum, filling up forms, interviewing parents, and devising end-of-term reports which shall combine a deep veneration for truth with a tender respect for the feelings of all concerned.

Sayers may have been speaking with her tongue firmly in her cheek, but the picture she paints is all too familiar to any schoolteacher. Educating at home, by contrast, presents parents with more opportunities to develop their children's natural sense of wonder. This doesn't mean simply opening the back door and tipping children into the garden, but it does mean making use of the freedom that home education provides. One educator who understood this perfectly was Charlotte Mason. Her approach to education is still hugely influential among many home educators, despite the fact that (or, perhaps, because) it was developed over a hundred years ago. Charlotte Mason believed in the importance of outdoor education, an idea which has now caught on in the educational mainstream, as the increasing popularity of forest schools reveals. She also wrote about the importance of living books, works of literature which could be enjoyed without being examined. For Charlotte Mason, education really is about drawing out the best in children rather than cramming information into them.

As I traveled around the country meeting home educators, I found a whole host of different approaches. Some families tend towards classical education; others follow a Charlotte Mason-inspired curriculum, while others still incorporate aspects of both. Some people call themselves traditionalists, others unschoolers, others still tidal homeschoolers. This last description is one of my favorites. Since home educators can respond more lithely to their children's needs and interests than any institution can, they can also adapt the model they use to suit different times of year and phases of their children's lives. Formal education can roll in and out like the tide on a sandy beach. We don't need to accept the industrial model of education that has dominated schools for the last 150 years.

As parents we have freedom, and freedom can sometimes scare us. That is why wisdom matters in education. We need to know how to use our freedom. We need to understand what freedom is. Many students in school understand it as freedom *from* constraints, whereas Christians see it as freedom *for* a greater good. That is why the notion of a preparation for freedom which some classical programs emphasize is so important. It's important for children and it's important for us too. Having been on the home education road for many years now, I know that we all still have much to learn, that none of us gets things completely right, but I've also come to realize that education is more like a track through the woods, forking in places, disappearing in others only to re-emerge in unexpected places, than it is like a train track. Not many of us know exactly where we are going when we start our home education journeys, but I for one am glad that we took the radical decision to set out on the way.

# 9

# L'Arche

IN THIS BOOK I have deliberately sought the good in radical Christianity. It's too easy to judge, to look for differences and then to condemn them. That is not the way towards spiritual growth. But it's also true that any exploration of radical Christianity needs to face up to hard questions and occasional betrayals. Openness to truth, goodness, and beauty, wherever they are found, does not mean we should close our eyes to abuses of power when we find them.

It was, for example, a real shock to discover, after spending some time visiting L'Arche, a community where people with learning disabilities live alongside those without such disabilities, that Jean Vanier, the organization's founder, had sexually abused a number of women under his spiritual care. Writing to the L'Arche Federation in 2020, the Leaders of L'Arche International expressed the sense of distress felt by many:

> We are shocked by these discoveries and unreservedly condemn these actions, which are in total contradiction with the values Jean Vanier otherwise stood for. They are incompatible with the basic rules of respect and dignity of persons, and contrary to the fundamental principles on which L'Arche is based. For many of us, Jean was one of the people we loved and respected the most. Jean inspired and comforted many people around the world … and we are aware that this information will cause many of us, both inside and outside L'Arche, deep confusion and pain. While the considerable good he did throughout his life is not in question, we will nevertheless have to mourn a certain image we may have had of Jean and of the origins of L'Arche.

# L'Arche

How, then, can we make sense of this terrible contradiction, that such evil could have been done by someone who was also capable of doing such good? It was a question I had to confront as I revisited L'Arche London. What I had considered another part of the journey turned out to be much more complicated: a double journey with one leg undertaken in the days before the revelations about Vanier's behavior came out and another in which I revisited that first journey in the light of what I now knew.

## Community life

I first came across L'Arche when a friend introduced me to Tim and Fiona Spargo-Mabbs, a remarkable couple who live and work for other people and are selfless in the gift they make of themselves, Fiona running a drugs-and-alcohol education charity and Tim working for L'Arche. When I told them about my travels in radical Christianity, Tim offered to introduce me to L'Arche London, an offer I readily accepted.

Though I didn't know a great deal about L'Arche, I did know a little about Tim and Fiona's sad personal history and wanted to understand how they could live for others when their own lives had been torn in two one night in January 2014. Dan Spargo-Mabbs, their younger son, was sixteen at the time, a popular, articulate, and engaging young man by all accounts. A regular churchgoer, he had recently signed up for a Youth Alpha course and seemed to have a bright future ahead of him. However, on that Friday night, having persuaded his mum to let him go to a party with friends, he went to an illegal rave instead where he succumbed to peer pressure and took Ecstasy. As his body temperature soared, his vital organs began to shut down and he was rushed to hospital in the early hours of the morning. On the following Monday he died, surrounded by his family. Less than a year later Dan's parents set up the Dan Spargo-Mabbs Foundation, explaining the foundation's purpose in this way:

> Dan was just 16 when he died. He was one of the very last people anyone would have expected to come to harm from drugs, but he did. Tim, Fiona and Jacob [Dan's older brother] felt if this could happen to someone like Dan, it could happen to anyone, and

they wanted to do all they could to prevent this. Dan's death is a tragedy that needn't have happened. The Daniel Spargo-Mabbs Foundation exists to make sure no harm happens to another young person through drugs or alcohol, and that all other young people get to go home safely.

Knowing all that, I also appreciated that an invitation from Tim to a L'Arche community supper would have a deep, emotional undercurrent. This wasn't just a job for him: it was a vocation that mattered more now than ever.

Meeting me at the station, Tim led me to the Portico Gallery, which I had imagined to be grander than it turned out to be. I'd been half-expecting an evening of fine art, funky furniture, and canapés, but the illusion evaporated the moment Tim directed me to a dimly lit side passage that led to a back room whose tiny red and green spotlights created the impression of a badly planned '70s disco. Inside, some fifty members of the L'Arche community were sitting around plastic trestle tables that wouldn't have been considered funky whatever light you saw them in. If the overall effect was of a subdued, old-school disco, the opening prayer also took me back to the '70s, when my main exposure to religion came from the Anglican primary school I attended in our village. The religious environment in which I grew up was defined by cheery, rather vacuous, choruses like "Think of a world without any flowers" and "Kumbaya," and new-fangled services like Christingle. Here in the Portico Gallery, we started the evening with an informal opening prayer followed by a curious hands-on ritual involving fruit and candles. I shifted uncomfortably in my seat, but we weren't done yet. As we sang a chorus and said more prayers, the voice of a middle-aged lady in a wheelchair boomed out, loudly but incoherently as she ululated in time to the music. No one appeared to mind apart from a slightly younger lady who stood with her back to the prayer leaders while the rest of us stood facing them. "Why's she making all that noise?" she asked loudly. I didn't hear the answer but whatever it was, it clearly didn't satisfy her, because she kept asking the same question over and over again until the singing, the prayers, and the ululations came to an end.

# L'Arche

Since Tim was busy running many of the evening's activities, my host for the evening was Richard, who had been a member of the community for many years but who lived on his own, maintaining a largely independent existence. He told me about some of his trips to L'Arche gatherings across the world and explained how the London community operated. Some of the community members need a lot of help, he explained, while others live in their own accommodation, joining the rest of the community for meals and other activities during the day. "The support I receive is mainly checking that I'm still alive and stuff like that," he told me.

**How to welcome the stranger**
Jean Vanier has described L'Arche not as a place but as a community of people: "We are people with and without intellectual disabilities living mutually transforming relationships in communities that become signs of peace in the world. We discover that, although some of us may have come to assist or help the core members, we too are changed. We become more patient, more kind, more accepting, more forgiving, more joyful." There seemed to be a great truth in these comments, even if they have been tarnished by later revelations about Vanier's character and actions. Certainly, I couldn't help contrasting the perception he expressed in this passage with my own inability to see beyond difference that evening. But L'Arche doesn't do difference. Or rather it embraces it. Whether Richard had an intellectual disability or not was unimportant. What mattered was that I was a guest and he was ready to welcome me.

One theologian has argued that welcoming lies at the heart of L'Arche's practical theology, since it values being and belonging over doing and having, welcome being "a sign of community life, the concretization of individual and communal trust in God's providence, and a conduit of God's presence in the world," as well as "a way of life inclined toward listening and remaining responsive to others; namely, God who is wholly Other, and then to other people."

I had come to L'Arche London wanting to talk and discovered that I had to listen. I had come expecting to see difference and had found a community where everyone has equal value. I had come with my head full of doing and soon realized that being was more important. As I relaxed, I began to enjoy myself, following the example of the lady who was sitting next to me at our table. She was clearly loving her meal, especially the cake, and, though she didn't have words to express that delight, her smile spoke for her. As she finished the slice on her plate, she reached across the table and nabbed a second piece from the plate of the young assistant opposite. Being in a wheelchair and having extremely limited mobility certainly didn't prevent her from pouncing with great dexterity. The assistant was none too amused but the rest of the table burst out laughing.

When the meal was over, we were treated to a presentation about forthcoming events and, more importantly, congratulated members of the community on their anniversaries at L'Arche. There was great delight as each face flashed up on the screen. Some of the people had been there for just a few years but others had been in the community for decades. None of them felt themselves to be members of an institution: this was home.

Even though I had only spent a very short time with the community, I looked with fresh eyes at my fellow passengers when I caught the train home that evening. They were mostly commuters, returning late from high-pressure jobs in the city. Most of them looked tired. Some of them seemed jaded. I couldn't help thinking that they were missing out on the fullness of life I had seen in the back room of the Portico Gallery. However, now that something of the L'Arche spirit had rubbed off on me, I couldn't stereotype them for long. They weren't merely commuters: they were people. People whose stories I did not know. Maybe that's a good definition of a stranger, I thought: someone whose stories we don't yet know.

### The reality of community life

It is easy to romanticize community life, a fact that Jean Vanier quickly came to appreciate: "From outside, community can seem such a beautiful place of sharing, cooperation, mutual support, and so on. But as soon as we are inside it, we quickly begin to see each others' faults!" We should neither romanticize the life we do not lead, he explained, nor become cynical simply because we do not share it: "We have to pass through these stages in order finally to

## L'Arche

meet people as they really are, neither angels nor demons, but human beings, beautiful and wounded, a mixture of light and darkness." There was more truth in that statement than I realized the first time I read it.

In the documentary film *Summer in the Forest*, Vanier explained that the early days of the growing community were times of great difficulty for him. Shortly after Vanier invited two men with intellectual disabilities, Raphael and Philippe, into his home, the director of the community known as Le Val Fleuri invited him to run it. Vanier jumped at the opportunity and tried to turn it from a place of anguish into a place of peace, but change came slowly. The brutalized men were often violent and windows were broken most days, which Vanier found hard to manage:

> I discovered something that I had never confronted before, that there were immense forces of darkness and hatred within my own heart. At particular moments of fatigue or stress, I saw forces of hate rising up inside me, and the capacity to hurt someone who was weak and provoking me!

Seeing Vanier at work in that film, it was hard to believe that he had hatred and darkness in his heart, but, as later became all too apparent, the truth is that no one is immune to the forces of sin and disorder. The real tragedy of Vanier's life is that he addressed some of the forces of darkness inside his own heart and ignored others, leaving the current leaders of L'Arche with a terribly divided legacy.

As I left L'Arche, I reflected on my own early experiences of community working at the night shelter in Leeds. As a twenty-one-year-old fresh from Oxford's ivory towers, I had no idea how to respond to the violence I experienced other than by keeping my head down and withdrawing from the men I was trying to help. Exposed to people I had previously always avoided, I came face to face with chronic alcoholism, drug abuse, and violent crime. I was also confronted by death shortly after one of our clients was admitted to hospital with acute liver failure. His funeral was the most depressing experience of my young life. Sitting in the crematorium chapel with the vicar and a couple of down-and-outs, I tried to make sense of how this man's life could have been so quickly forgotten, how he could have passed away with scarcely a whimper. I learned a great deal about homelessness during that year, but all I learned about myself was that I wanted nothing more to do with challenging men and violent situations. That's why I started a PhD, moving on from the night shelter with scarcely a backwards glance.

Now, however, many years later, as I reflected on what I had seen in L'Arche London (and also in the Franciscan Friars of the Renewal's soup kitchen), I started to reappraise my youthful experiences. My attitudes, I realized, were not so different from the young Jean Vanier's. Some of what he wrote could have been said about me:

> Looking back, I can see that when I was in the navy I was preoccupied with success and with trying to win the admiration of my superiors. I loved the spirit and power that came with naval life. Efficiency, not people, was my first concern. Similarly, when I left the navy, it was not primarily *people* who interested me. I wanted to devote myself to an *ideal* of peace and Christian life, and to the study of philosophy and theology. Certainly, I wanted to follow Jesus, to know him and love him, but more out of idealism than because I wanted to live in communion. It took me some time to discover all my inner brokenness, which provoked difficulties in relationships and a fear of others. I was happy to command, teach, obey, and learn; but entering into communion with others, making myself vulnerable by forming relationships with them, was far more difficult. I avoided people by throwing my energy into doing good things, praying and studying. But maybe that was a necessary time of growth for me. I needed the spiritual and intellectual formation which would gradually give me the inner strength to be able to enter into real relationships, to learn to listen to people and love them, and to become really myself.

What I had lacked as a young man, I was beginning to realize, was a sense of communion with the homeless men I met. I wanted to do things for them but I certainly had no idea that I might be able to learn from them. I had a dim sense that I might be able to solve their problems but no idea that what was required of me was to walk with them. "For many people in pain there is no solution," Jean Vanier wrote, adding that when "a child has experienced rejec-

## L'Arche

tion, you can say all sorts of nice things to the child, but that will not take away the pain. It will take a long time for that pain to diminish and it will probably never completely disappear."

Twenty-five years after working in the night shelter, I now knew this to be true. As the father of two adopted children, I had gradually learned that our task as parents was not to ignore our children's "primal wound" (as Nancy Newton Verrier has called it) or attempt to erase it, but to be there for them and with them, knowing that the slow processes of love would diminish the pain that came from their early traumatic experiences, even if it wouldn't remove it completely. Slowly I had learned that it was only love that would enable our children to become fully themselves, which meant that I had to lay aside hundreds of unspoken assumptions about what parents do. Above all else, I had discovered that I needed to listen to our children, especially when they weren't talking. Reading about Jean Vanier's experiences gave me a severe jolt that made me focus not so much on his life as on my own:

> When there is communion between people, they sometimes work together, but what matters to them is not that they succeed in achieving some target, but simply that they are together, that they find their joy in one another and care for one another. Raphael and Philippe really led me into this world of communion. When I was in the navy, I did not seek to enter into communion with the men under my command. I gave them orders. I was superior to them. If they failed in some way or found themselves in difficulties, I had either to try to resolve their problems or to reprimand them. When I was a teacher, I had to tell the students what they needed to do or learn; I had to correct their work, to inspire them intellectually. With Raphael and Philippe, what was needed was to create a warm atmosphere where we could be bonded together in love and in mutual commitment, and where we could live in communion with each other as if we were a family.

### The community of the family

Ever since my visit to the Bruderhof community, I have been seeking a way for families to become part of communities that can, in turn, strengthen those families as they seek to resist the siren voices of secular liberalism. (And if that search seems familiar, I have to confess that this book has all along been in implicit, if tangential, dialogue with Rod Dreher's *Benedict Option*.) However, there's another way of seeing the same journey, as a search for ways in which communities can become more like families, for ways of understanding the family as itself already a community, a place where, sometimes slowly and painfully, we edge away from "the community for myself" towards "myself for the community." The farther I traveled, the more it seemed that our goal ought to be true communion, whether that communion was found in a family or in some other kind of community.

Without realizing it, we had already set out on this path as a family. Drawing on the fierce love that parents have for their children, we have gradually learned to live life differently, no longer accepting the assumptions of our modern, secular, liberal, consumerist society, while not yet managing to wholly escape the lures it constantly throws our way. I had set out on my travels in search of radical Christianity and discovered that I needed radical change within. I knew my love for my children and could honestly say that I have learned to learn from them, but I didn't know whether I was prepared to take what I had begun to learn in the family into the wider community. As I came face-to-face with the uncomfortable realities that L'Arche and its deeply flawed founder presented me with, I started to ask myself some hard questions. Was I throwing myself into work so I could block out the rest of the world? Was I avoiding communion with the weak and marginalized by immersing myself in writing and academic work?

Christmas was rapidly approaching as I wrestled with these questions, so I decided to take my children to the L'Arche London nativity play. It was quite an experience. Arriving early, we found that some last-minute coaching was still going on behind the scenes. Mary, in particular, was having trouble remembering her lines: "When he asks, you say, 'Yes,'" a disembodied voice said. I don't think they realized the microphones had been left on. In the row in front of us, a young lady with Down Syndrome was clearly not looking forward to the performance. "I don't want to go, I don't

## L'Arche

want to go," she kept telling her mother. In the end, a kind assistant led her up onto the stage so she could join the rest of the angelic chorus. Meanwhile a few angels, wise men, and other unidentified characters were walking around, chatting to friends and getting ready for the show. My children didn't quite know what to make of it. However, the play eventually began with Richard leading us through the action as one of two narrators.

It would be easy to distract you with details—the workmen visiting the infant Jesus or the wise men arriving by train—but what really hit home that day was that this play about the poor and dispossessed was being performed by the poor and dispossessed. People with disabilities acted alongside people without disabilities. No distinctions were made and none were necessary. At the end of the performance, a hesitant young angel danced for joy in front of the angelic chorus and Mary beamed with happiness. The legacy of Jean Vanier was ambiguous at best but here at least was an unambiguous good.

Having seen the nativity play, I knew it was time to move on, to seek inspiration once more in the lives of others. There were many more communities of radical Christians I could have visited, but it now seemed clear to me that there was much more to radical Christianity than the life of counter-cultural communities. As I walked my children back to the car, I realized that the next stage of my journey had to have a different focus. It was time to visit Margaret and Barry Mizen.

# 10

# Margaret and Barry Mizen

MARGARET AND BARRY MIZEN are two of the most remarkable people I have ever met and am ever likely to meet, so I was delighted to have the opportunity to see them again. Approaching their home in Lee from the north, I passed a curious mixture of shops, cafés, and pubs: Bubble Stop, the Rhubarb and Custard Café, Tattooooze, The Old Tiger's Head, and even, incongruously, the Museum of Neo-Liberalism. Turning into Burnt Ash Road, which eventually becomes Burnt Ash Hill, I passed Edith Nesbit's old house in Dorville Road and the Tolkienian-sounding Micheldever Road on the right before driving under the railway line to a small row of shops. It was here, in a former bakery, now a café, that Margaret and Barry's son Jimmy was murdered in an unprovoked attack on May 10, 2008, the day after his sixteenth birthday. Jimmy Mizen was the thirteenth teenager to be killed in London that year and the media were ready to move on because teenage deaths were no longer headline news, but Margaret and Barry's response to their son's murder changed all that. Before the weekend was over, Jimmy's name was appearing in newspaper headlines across the world.

I first met Barry and Margaret when they spoke to students at my school. I've heard many inspirational talks over the years, but the inspiration usually fades with time. This talk was different. What struck me then, and what continues to impress me to this day, was the way in which these two ordinary people (as they are happy to describe themselves) were able to respond in such an extraordinary way to the horror that was unleashed on their family that Saturday morning in May.

Having turned sixteen, Jimmy told his parents that he wanted to buy his first lottery ticket. Then, with one of his brothers, he walked to a local shop to buy his lottery ticket before going to a nearby baker's shop. While they were waiting to be served, a local lad with a history of violence walked in. Knowing this and having been mugged by him before, Jimmy and his brother were keen to avoid a confrontation. Unfortunately, he didn't feel the same way. Very quickly he lost his temper and had to be forced out of the shop. He then broke his way back in and threw a glass bowl at Jimmy with such force that it shattered on impact, a piece of glass piercing Jimmy's neck, severing an artery and partially severing his jugular vein. As the murderer ran away, Jimmy tried to escape to the back of the shop, where he shut himself in a cupboard. It was there that another of his brothers found him. Shortly afterwards Jimmy died in his arms.

How does any parent deal with a horror like that? How can anyone not give way to the power of destructive emotions in such circumstances? No one would have condemned the Mizens if they had expressed anger, hatred, and a burning desire for vengeance. But they didn't. That afternoon, they went back home to find two hundred people in their house, all of whom had come to offer what support and consolation they could. Needing to make sense of what had just happened and still reeling from the sudden loss of her son, Margaret retreated to the quiet of her bedroom. There she made Jimmy two promises: that she and Barry would keep Jimmy's name alive and that they would dedicate their lives to working for peace. It was a remarkable promise to make so soon after Jimmy had been taken from them.

The day after Jimmy's murder, Barry and Margaret attended Mass at their parish church, Our Lady of Lourdes. Barry was down to be Eucharistic Minister that day and, though he could easily have stepped aside, he decided that he wanted to serve as normal. "I was holding the chalice at Holy Communion time," he later wrote, "and people were coming up to me weeping. My shirt was wet through with their tears. Yet I was so calm. It was strange." Margaret was strangely calm too, telling reporters after Mass that her prayers were with the family of the murderer, adding, "I can't, I don't feel anger." A week later, at a memorial service for Jimmy, she said, "Anger breeds anger and bitterness, and bitterness will destroy my family if

I'm not careful—and I won't allow that to happen." That was not the message that the media were expecting to hear.

Time and time again in the days and weeks after their son's murder, Margaret and Barry spoke words of peace and hope. How was that possible? When I asked them that question, they seemed almost as baffled as everyone else. They said that they didn't sit down and plan what to say. In fact, they had no experience of dealing with the press at all. But when they started speaking, it was a message of peace and hope which emerged. They also told me that it was their faith that sustained them during those terrible days and it was their faith that enabled them to speak as they did when the world's reporters flocked to their door. "Undoubtedly, we said the words that we did because God was working in our lives," Margaret told me. "I don't doubt that for a minute because if you had said to me the day before Jimmy was killed, 'Margaret, if someone hurt one of your children, what would you do?' I'd have said, like many parents, 'I'll kill them if they do anything to my children.' And yet someone took the life of my son and I was speaking words of peace, words of hope."

What sustained Barry and Margaret at that time was prayer and an assurance that Jimmy was in heaven. Speaking to a crowd of 80,000 people in Hyde Park during Pope Benedict XVI's visit to Britain in 2010, Margaret described retreating to her bedroom on the day of Jimmy's murder in this way: "The only thing I could think of was that my son was now in heaven with God. I felt the real presence of the Lord there and prayed and prayed the Hail Mary and the Our Father and I knew that Jimmy was safe. The pain was unbearable but we got through those awful times, particularly the next couple of days. But to this day I still know my son is safe in heaven."

Margaret and Barry are not conspicuously pious people but they don't hide their faith either: "I always said I would stand up for my faith," Margaret told me, "but never knew if I would." It is obvious that prayer and an intimate relationship with God sustained them in the weeks after their son's death and sustains them to this day. As Margaret put it when speaking to the Hyde Park crowd, "I can tell you now, had I not been able to speak words of love, God's words, I wouldn't have coped. If God hadn't been in my life, I wouldn't have coped. Through all the deepest, darkest moments of losing Jimmy,

## Margaret and Barry Mizen

I've prayed. And I usually pray with my husband and we often hold each other tight. We still to this day cry, but we will pray and pray and pray. Our prayers are what sustained us, what allowed us to get up each day and do the things that we're doing."

### Permission to love

Their first invitation to speak in a school came shortly after Jimmy's death, and it didn't take long before the invitations started to roll in from prisons and police training colleges as well. Since Barry owned a shoe repair shop and Margaret was a stay-at-home mum to their nine children, neither of them had public speaking experience. Being invited to speak in public was daunting, so they decided to speak from the heart, telling their story simply and directly. Barry told me that whenever he tried to plan what to say the words wouldn't come right, but whenever he trusted the Holy Spirit, everything fell into place. "They say God uses blunt instruments," he joked. "Well, you can't get any more blunt than me."

One of the people who was hit hardest by their words and actions was Barnie Choudhury, the BBC journalist who scooped the first interview with the grieving couple. Hearing about the impact the Mizens had had on him, I contacted Barnie to ask him about his experiences. The effusiveness of the answer he gave took me by surprise. Hardened hacks don't usually open up to complete strangers, nor do they allow the stories they're covering to affect them emotionally. But this was no ordinary story and Barnie Choudhury, it turned out, was no hardened hack. Here's how he described the events of those few days:

> I know it was a long time ago, but my meeting with Margaret and Barry will be forever etched into my soul. We got the shout just after 4 pm. I was the weekend correspondent for the BBC, and I was used to reporting on the tragic killings of teenagers in London.
>
> On this hot May day, I travelled with the camera crew to the Three Cooks Bakery in Burnt Ash Hill, south London. The police had put cordons around the crime scene, and as ever my role was to gather news. I went on air about fifteen minutes after

I arrived, and the late and wonderful Peter Sissons interviewed me for a two-way. After that I spoke to people, and we had everything we needed for the late Saturday evening news.

As I called the news desk in to say I was leaving, the news organizer said that I should go and get reaction from Jimmy's parents. In the trade it's called the "death knock," of which I had done scores in my twenty-plus-year career. This is crass at the best of times.

"How are you feeling?" asks the stupid reporter.

"How do think, you blithering moron?" comes the response.

I turned to my camera crew and said, "I'm not doing it. These poor parents have just lost their son. Let them grieve. We'll drive past the house, and they won't be in."

I wasn't suggesting, I was saying we weren't going to disturb the parents. Luckily, my colleague agreed and got it immediately.

I know why I did this. Our daughter, Olivia, was 11 and in a few weeks, she would turn 12. I wouldn't see her until Tuesday morning because I was in London, and she was safely at home with her mother in Leicester. All I wanted to do was give my little girl a hug and let her know how much I loved her, keep her safe—something Barry and Margaret wouldn't be able to do. Many journalists would think I was being unprofessional. I disagree. My approach has always been: people first—story second. My other axiom is that things happen for a reason.

The next day the news organizer, Laurie Margolis, sent me back. Press Association, a trusted news agency, reported Barry and Margaret were at church and they had spoken. I breathed a sigh of relief and felt better about what I was going to do.

Barry and Margaret hadn't returned from church, so I did what I always did, knocked on their neighbor's home. He was a guy called Rob who had young children and was effusive. I remember he welcomed us in and explained Barry and Margaret weren't at home, but we could wait. Memory is a funny thing—Rob offered us tea, but he said he didn't have milk because his children could only drink soya. About thirty minutes later, and we'd made all the small talk we could, Rob spotted Margaret and Barry had returned.

## Margaret and Barry Mizen

I said, "Look, I don't want to intrude on their grief, please would you mind letting them know we're here—and if they don't want to speak, we'll be on our way—absolutely no pressure."

Five minutes later, Barry and Margaret walked through the front door.

You could spot the strain immediately—and again my heart skipped more than one beat, and I had to steel myself. Here was an ordinary couple, and I was about to pretend to be a friend and ask them to bare their souls. It's my job, right?

Then Margaret spoke.

"Thank you so much for what you said about my Jimmy," she began, "you made him come alive and I don't know how you did that."

In all my years of broadcast journalism, I had never met anyone who had my immediate respect.

We were seated in Rob's kitchen, and I explained what I'd like to do, but they were under no pressure to speak with me. But for some inexplicable reason, Barry and Margaret agreed. I'm not sure I could have—and although this has happened to me so many times, I am surprised every time someone wants to talk to absolute strangers about tragic moments. I expected the interview to last for five minutes tops, and I'd need to check, but I'm pretty sure it lasted for at least fifteen minutes.

Throughout, I wanted to cry, but I must have gone into autopilot. I wanted to put a reassuring blanket around this incredibly brave couple. Margaret said she felt sorry for the killer's family and that her prayers are with them. Wow. I couldn't do that.

Because I knew it was for television, I asked whether they had any moving images of Jimmy—and they did. It was video of Jimmy dancing—and it was something which showed what might have been.

I did a series of live broadcasts that day, and I knew I had probably met two people who would influence me forever. How? Well, they showed kindness and compassion in the act of evil. They showed the capacity to forgive. They taught me to be kinder. They gave me permission to love my only child even more than I did, and to live every moment telling her she was the center of our lives.

I'm no saint, but when I'm having a bad day, I realize how lucky I am, and remembering the Mizens makes me feel better.

Margaret and Barry continue to touch people's lives. Their work is inspiring. Their faith in their God is unimaginable. Every day they use tragedy and adversity as the points from which to demonstrate true love towards others. Quite remarkable. They're not zealots, I don't think. They're not preachy. By sharing their story, they do so much good, and I wish there were more Barrys and Margarets in the world. I know I was blessed to meet them.

My final two stories are from the Monday. I was asked by BBC Breakfast for their phone number. I was asked by Victoria Derbyshire's team for their number. I had it, but I refused to share it. Not because I wanted to keep it to myself, but simply because I know the news machine. Sometimes, just sometimes, we need to take a step back and be human, or as Harper Lee's Atticus Finch said to Scout, his daughter, in *To Kill A Mockingbird*, "You never really understand a person until you consider things from his point of view . . . until you climb in his skin and walk around in it." It's something I have taught a generation of students I have had the privilege to teach.

People first. Story second. Trust people. Have humanity.

I was sent back that Monday, but I asked the news organizer to put someone else on the story. We came to a compromise—I would do lives while my colleague Ben Ando would work for the One, Six and Ten.

When I tell this story to colleagues, they think I'm mad because every journalist wants to be on the flagship BBC television news programs. I just didn't want to do the story three days running because I knew I was in danger of saying something stupid. I wanted to go live and say, "This is why the government's useless. This is why we need tougher laws. This is why we need to put resources into educating young people and giving them hope, not closing down community centers and cutting back on resources."

## Margaret and Barry Mizen

Anyway, I went, and did a few lives. My heart wasn't in it. As ever, the media were moving to their next story and the circus would soon be out of town, and the news organizer told me I could go home. As I did so, I popped across to the Mizens' home and rang the doorbell.

Barry answered, and I said I wanted to say goodbye in case we didn't see one another again, and I wanted to pass on my condolences once again.

Barry came forward and gave me a hug, and I dissolved in tears—something I have never done before or since on a story. I knew it was the right time to leave frontline reporting.

Two years later, I left the BBC and became a leader, and I hope I have led with compassion and humanity. That remains the legacy of my meeting an ordinary couple who proved to be extraordinary.

### Forgiveness, peace, and hope

From that terrible weekend onwards, Barry and Margaret have been witnesses to God's mysterious love, but it took them time to process what had happened to their family. In the early days, the punchbag in their garden got plenty of use, and it was a long time before Barry was able to even mention the name of Jimmy's murderer, but over time he found he was able to say he forgave him, and over time he and Margaret together discovered what it was that God wanted them to do with their lives.

That togetherness is important. "Trauma breaks relationships," they said, but they remained strongly united. Time and time again in our conversation, they mentioned the importance of prayer. "We feel very comfortable praying together," Margaret said, adding that in those days they were "crying and crying and crying, and praying and praying and praying." Reflecting on their life and work, Barry also suggested that their experiences as parents of a daughter with Down Syndrome had, in some sense, helped prepare them for the work they have done since Jimmy's death. Discovering that their daughter had Downs was a shock to them at first, but they soon threw themselves into supporting other parents as well as caring for their own children, setting up a local support group for families of children with Down Syndrome. What they learned then was an idea that has continued to sustain them: "The strong need the weak."

Barry and Margaret certainly weren't prepared for the invitations they received to speak about their experiences soon after Jimmy's death, but, looking back, they now see that God had given them the tools they needed to speak about forgiveness, peace, and hope. It is impossible to say where exactly they found the inner strength that enabled them to turn away from hatred and embrace a message soaked in love, but, on a human level, their motivation seems largely to have come from the desire to protect their children, to hold their family together. "I had the need to smile again," Margaret said, "to see the sunshine." If Jimmy's death had destroyed her, it would have destroyed her family too.

What Barry discovered at Mass the day after Jimmy died has continued to be true in the years since then: other people need them. "It's almost as if we're specialists in death," he said. "So we give other people support." That means helping care for other parents who have lost their children to violence, but the support they give extends far beyond that. As they soon discovered, having the ability to forgive allowed them to reach out across apparently impassable barriers. "I hold murderers in my arms," Margaret told me. Even knowing what I now know about the Mizens, I was taken aback by that statement. It would be an amazing thing for anyone to say; for someone whose son has been murdered, it is almost incomprehensible.

Didn't they ever question their faith in the aftermath of Jimmy's death? I asked them. "Why would we let go of God at the moment we needed Him?" Margaret replied. Barry agreed, telling me about a time he had read a passage from the Bible he found in *Magnificat*, a devotional publication including daily Mass readings and prayers. "It was almost as if it was leaping off the page," he said. "And God was saying, 'Use it.'" A few years ago Margaret was diagnosed with cancer, but again she and Barry turned to God rather than away from Him during that difficult time. "It was prayers got us through it," she said.

The Mizens have come through challenges that would sink many families and they have gained a vibrant, selfless faith in the process.

## Margaret and Barry Mizen

The complexity of the challenges they have faced was potentially debilitating, but they have instead been able to hold on to what truly matters: forgiveness, peace, and hope, three simple words which lie at the heart of everything they now say and do. "We talk about forgiveness in a way people can understand," Barry said. At its heart, their message is very simple. Forgiveness matters because, without it, life simply isn't possible. But it's not so much the words they speak that matter: it's the fact that they have practiced forgiveness in their own lives that speaks to so many people. In a similar way, hope has sustained them through the darkest times. "This world needs hope," Margaret told me. "Hope is such a beautiful word." And then there's the peace that so many communities are calling out for in our broken, atomized society, the peace Margaret and Barry were determined to work for in memory of Jimmy. To understand the power of their work in this area, we need to take a step back to the weeks after Jimmy's murder.

### Safe spaces

What soon became clear from my conversation with the Mizens is that they have a remarkable capacity for listening to God and responding to His promptings. When I asked about the development of their charitable work, they told me that they simply responded to events. What God wanted of them slowly emerged over time. They didn't take matters into their own hands but listened and allowed God to work through them. "God is entwined in all of it, in everything we do," Margaret said.

The news cycle moves on very quickly, but reporters came back to see the Mizens every now and again: at Jimmy's memorial service a week after his murder; at his funeral two months later; on the day he posthumously received his high school examination results. On this occasion Margaret and Barry made sandwiches for the journalists and continued to speak about peace. Later that same year they received their first invitation to speak to school students, though their charitable work had already begun on a small scale as they joined a local scout group in collecting money to buy a bus. University students contributed £100; then money started arriving through the post, sometimes simply labelled "Jimmy" and containing a few coins. By the end of the year they had enough to buy the Twenty-First Lewisham North Scouts a seventeen-seater minibus and were well on their way to buying a second bus for another scout group.

Over time their charitable work developed into a charity, For Jimmy. They created a Safe Havens program as a direct response to the events that had led to Jimmy's murder. They persuaded shops and other public spaces to provide safe spaces for anyone who felt threatened, a Safe Haven sticker in their window signaling this place of refuge. A step up from these safe havens were the Good Hope Cafés which started to open two years after Jimmy's death. These cafés brought in funds for the charity but were also safe spaces in their own right. They also provided opportunities for Margaret and Barry to help young people in south London. Before long they were employing youngsters, providing work experience, and offering personalized placements for young people on the autism spectrum. With that solid base in place, all sorts of other events and activities were able to spring up, including children's groups, comedy nights, and film screenings.

After a talk Margaret gave in the school where I worked, a group of sixth-form students began to meet and plan ways in which they could help. I took them to one of the Good Hope Cafés, where they met members of the family and learned more about the work of the charity. Then Margaret and Barry set them a task. Could they help design a workpack for the primary schools that were now inviting Margaret and Barry in to talk? Rather than hear a talk and then move on, could these young children explore the message of forgiveness, peace, and hope in practical ways to become change-makers in the world? My students set to work and eventually came up with a series of suggestions which they presented to the Mizens. Working with Margaret and Barry certainly had a big impact on my students. Like so many others, they came away from that encounter as better people.

The Mizens poured themselves into their charity work and achieved much success. So it was all the more heartbreaking when they found that they and the charity's trustees were beginning to pull in different directions. Eventually, things became so bad that they had to step away from the charity they had founded. "It was almost as painful as when we lost Jimmy," Margaret told me. Yet again they were facing a challenge with which many people would have struggled to cope, but their faith remained strong and, out of the ashes of that charity, a new, smaller charity, the Mizen Foundation, emerged. The good work goes on.

**Small deeds done are better than great deeds planned**
Sitting in their living room, I asked Margaret and Barry about the latest challenge they have had to face, the recent release of Jimmy's murderer from prison on parole. "We've come to terms with it," Barry said. Conditions have been attached to his release, including an exclusion order, but his parents still live just up the road. It's clearly not an easy situation. Nonetheless, as they have done over and over again in difficult times, Margaret and Barry are focusing on the good they can do, not on the difficulties they face.

They are now familiar faces in places as varied as Millwall Football Club and Buckingham Palace. They have received MBEs for their work, Margaret is Pro-Chancellor of St Mary's University, they've had tea with Prince Charles and spoken to 80,000 people in Hyde Park when Pope Benedict XVI came to Britain ("I know what the scaffold at Tyburn must have felt like," Barry commented), but they are also keen to point out that they are just ordinary people; "we're just Barry and Margaret, for goodness sake," Barry said with a smile. He had a point, but what strikes anyone who meets Margaret and Barry for the first time is that they are ordinary people doing extraordinary things. They have the most wonderful ability to see the good in people. They are warm and welcoming. They love life. Spending any amount of time with them is a truly enriching experience.

As I got up to go, Barry went off to find a quotation he liked. "I've found it," he said, as Margaret opened the front door. "Small deeds done are better than great deeds planned." It's true, I thought as I drove back home, but it's also true that small deeds soon become great deeds when done by people like Margaret and Barry.

# 11

# Radical Orthodoxy

HAVING SPENT SOME TIME with Margaret and Barry Mizen, I could see that my travels were coming to an end. The restlessness which had set me off in the first place was abating, mainly because I now had so much inspiration on which to draw. However, there were still some issues which needed addressing before I could unpack my traveling bag, one of which had been bugging me ever since I first read *The Benedict Option*.

In that book, Rod Dreher argued that "serious Christian conservatives could no longer live business-as-usual lives in America, that we have to develop creative, communal solutions to help us hold on to our faith and our values in a world growing ever more hostile to them. We would have to choose to make a decisive leap into a truly countercultural way of living Christianity, or we would doom our children and our children's children to assimilation." Dreher's book has been hugely influential, but was he right? That was the question I had been asking myself throughout my travels. And, if he was, what did that mean for me, for my family, and for Christians not just in America but around the world?

The impact of Dreher's book has certainly been widely felt. It has also had its critics. Writing in *First Things*, for example, R.R. Reno argued that "there's something very right about Rod Dreher's call to action in *The Benedict Option: A Strategy for Christians in a Post-Christian Nation*. He urges us to ask if we have 'compromised too much with the world' and suggests ways to renew the integrity of our religious communities. Yet there's also something wrong. A rhetoric of crisis runs through *The Benedict Option*. The dire picture of our present challenges is likely to confuse Christians rather than help us discern the way forward." It is this language of crisis with which Reno disagrees: "The rhetorical structure of *The Benedict Option* requires imminent disaster. Thus it's not surprising that Dreher is drawn to the flood as the fitting biblical image for our time. The storm is coming. There's no escape but . . . the Benedict Option." Reno argues instead that "we have not 'lost on every front'" and that "our times are like every other historical epoch between Christ's ascension into heaven and his return in glory: a complicated combination of good and bad trends." Challenges there certainly are, but not an existential threat to the Church in the West. According to Reno, "we are not living in a singular age in which Christianity must become a counter-culture. The Sermon on the Mount frames a way of life *that always has been a counter-culture.*"

So how should we respond to the challenges of our times? One answer is to return to the book that inspired Rod Dreher, Alasdair MacIntyre's *After Virtue,* and especially to the rhetorical flourish with which he finishes in comparing our age with the last days of the Roman Empire in the West:

> A crucial turning point . . . occurred when men and women of good will turned aside from the task of shoring up the Roman *imperium* and ceased to identify the continuation of civility and moral community with the maintenance of that *imperium*. What they set themselves to achieve instead—often not recognizing fully what they were doing—was the construction of new forms of community within which the moral life could be sustained so that both morality and civility might survive the coming ages of barbarism and darkness. If my account of our moral condition is correct, we ought to conclude that for some time now we too have reached that turning point. What matters at this stage is the construction of local forms of community within which civility and the intellectual and moral life can be sustained through the new dark ages which are already upon us. And if the tradition of the virtues was able to survive the horrors of the last dark ages, we are not entirely without grounds for hope. This time however the barbarians are not waiting beyond the frontiers, they have already been governing us for some time. And it is our lack of consciousness of this that constitutes part of our predicament. We are waiting not for a Godot, but for another—doubtless very different—St Benedict.

*Travels in Radical Christianity*

**Ask Rowan**

What would St Benedict have made of the times in which we are living? What might it mean to be another, very different, St Benedict today? Dreher's book provides partial answers to those questions, but he is not the only person to have been inspired by *After Virtue*, and so I decided to investigate what others have said about being radical, being counter-cultural, today. An obvious place to start was with the Radical Orthodoxy movement.

I first became acquainted with Radical Orthodoxy when I started a PhD in theology several years ago. More than several years ago, in fact. While going on my travels in radical Christianity, I had also found myself on a quest for a doctorate that had become something of an epic journey in its own right. Over the years I have started PhDs in history at Cambridge, in children's literature at De Montfort University, and in theology at the John Paul II Institute for Family and Marriage in Melbourne, Australia, but not managed to finish any of them. (I also once applied for a place at Reading University to study the ways in which the novels of Robert Westall have been read and understood, but pursued the application no further when I realized that my main motivation was wanting to tell people that I was reading reading at Reading.) However, having transferred to the University of Nottingham, the epicenter of Radical Orthodoxy, when the JPII Institute closed, I was confident that my doctoral travels were at last drawing to an end.

My supervisor at Nottingham is Alison Milbank. We usually meet for supervisions online, because Nottingham, though closer than Australia, is still some considerable distance from my home. My first experience of meeting Alison's husband, John Milbank, who launched the Radical Orthodoxy movement, was therefore slightly surreal. We were having an online supervision about *Laurus*, a brilliant novel by the Ukrainian-Russian novelist Eugene Vodolazkin, and were struggling over a particular interpretation when suddenly a disembodied voice boomed out across the ether: "Ask Rowan!" It was John Milbank, and the Rowan to whom he was referring was Rowan Williams, the former Archbishop of Canterbury.

John Milbank's presence still hovers dramatically over the Radical Orthodoxy movement which he founded with Graham Ward

## Radical Orthodoxy

and Catherine Pickstock in Cambridge during the 1990s. Milbank's ideas, especially as expressed in his seminal book *Theology and Social Theory*, have influenced a huge number of people from Catholic, Protestant, and Orthodox backgrounds, ranging from William T. Cavanaugh, Stanley Hauerwas, Michael Hanby, and David Bentley Hart in the USA to Charles Taylor in Canada, Rowan Williams, Fergus Kerr, Conor Cunningham, and Adrian Pabst in the UK, and Tracey Rowland, my former supervisor, in Australia, to name but a few. Could they help me, I wondered, as I tried to make sense of the journeys I had been on? Could they provide me with a way of understanding the task of radical Christianity today? Did they confirm the analyses of Rod Dreher or suggest another way of responding to our contemporary predicaments?

My first step was to get to grips with *Theology and Social Theory* and its provocative opening words: "Once there was no 'secular.'" Milbank's point is not that we now live in a secular age whereas we once lived in an age of faith. Rather, he is arguing that the very terms we use to describe our current age are loaded. It is very modern to believe that there are two distinct spheres: the secular and the religious. That distinction would have made no sense to people a thousand—even five hundred—years ago. It is now widely believed that a value-free science explains the world and that religion is an optional extra which can provide either solace or private values but nothing more. Religion should be tolerated as long as it remains firmly hidden in the private sphere: it should not impose itself on the public realm of politics, business, or law. Of course, the argument goes, there are still many religious believers but they are on their way out. An inevitable process of secularization is slowly destroying religious belief as the powers of science and reason sweep away old superstitions.

Though still widely touted—especially by a now dwindling band of New Atheists—this understanding of the modern age has fallen out of favor in the academic world. As many thinkers have pointed out, neither science nor reason is value-free or neutral, and the notion of inevitable secularization simply doesn't fit the facts. As Simon Oliver, now Professor of Divinity at Durham, puts it:

This view of the transformation from the mediaeval consensus to the modern secular world is so straightforward that we often take it for granted. It is a view which sees the secular as the result of clearing away the debris of superstition, ritual and tradition which we imagine dominated mediaeval Europe to open new possibilities directed by the neutral hand of reason expressed most particularly in the natural sciences. The advent of the secular is therefore seen as the natural result of the inevitable progress of human knowledge and thinking.

However, Oliver continues, this view simply doesn't hold together:

Milbank's crucial point is that the secular is not simply the rolling back of a theological consensus to reveal a neutral territory where we all become equal players, but the replacement of a certain view of God and creation with a different view which still makes theological claims, that is, claims about origins, purpose and transcendence. The problem is that this "mock-theology" or "pseudo-theology" is bad theology. Secularism is, quite literally, a Christian heresy—an ideological distortion of theology.

Once there was no secular and there was no religion either. "Religion" is a baggy catch-all term that has been turned into a useful bugbear by Richard Dawkins and his New Atheist friends. Turning abruptly from Southern Baptists to traditional Catholics to fundamentalist Muslims, Dawkins fires at the first target he sees and then claims he has slain a great monster. However, the truth of the matter, as William T. Cavanaugh has written, is that "there is no transhistorical or transcultural concept of religion essentially separate from politics. Religion has a history, and what counts as religion and what does not in any given context depends on different configurations of power and authority." What's more, he points out, any attempt to deny this is a sure sign of a secularizing agenda: "The attempt to say that there *is* a transhistorical and transcultural concept of religion that is separable from secular phenomena *is itself* part of a particular configuration of power, that of the modern, liberal nation-state as it developed in the West."

What John Milbank attempted to do in *Theology and Social Theory*, then, was not to save "religion" but to reclaim Theology as the queen of the sciences; to demonstrate that it isn't a fringe subject for a few quirky eccentrics who have nothing better to do, but the means by which we can best understand the whole of reality. As he used to tell graduate students at Cambridge when asked about his area of specialization, "I am interested in everything and in the God who is beyond everything." For Milbank and Radical Orthodoxy, the counter-cultural task that Christians have today is not to retreat from the public sphere but to reclaim it, confident that radically orthodox theology gives us the ability to transform the world by rooting out bad theology masquerading as value-free secular reason and replacing it with a transformative participation in the life of God Himself.

**Radical and Orthodox**

But what might the good theology replacing the heresy of secularism actually look like? In a world riven by denominational differences, how can we possibly find common ground from which to launch a counter-cultural offensive? The answer that Radical Orthodoxy gives takes us back beyond the denominational divisions of the last thousand years to a time when Christians in East and West were still doctrinally united. It is a radical movement because, like the *ressourcement* thinkers of the twentieth century, it asks us to return to our theological roots, and it is orthodox because it draws its theology from a time when there was still only one faith, when all Christians agreed what it meant to be orthodox. The founders of Radical Orthodoxy may have been high Anglicans who all worshipped in the same church in Cambridge, but their theology is rooted in the work of writers who lived before the Faith had even arrived in England.

There is a danger, of course, that this all sounds abstractly intellectual, but the reality is that Radically Orthodox (or RO) thinkers find themselves at the forefront of debates about evolutionary theory, modern physics, post-liberal politics, and a whole host of other currently pressing issues. By drawing on our collective Christian roots and a faith that is truly orthodox, thinkers in the Radical Orthodoxy tradition have cut through tired theological debates and forged a new path for renewal in the Church.

*Travels in Radical Christianity*

One key aspect of RO's work is its analysis of our views of God. It traces the growth of secularism back to theological mistakes made hundreds of years ago, to distorted understandings of God and His relationship to his creation which crept into theology with the work of Duns Scotus and others in the thirteenth and fourteenth centuries. The RO critique of Duns Scotus is complex, but what it boils down to is that, after Scotus, people tended to see humans and God on a continuum: "God now has a more intense and infinite being which is possessed to a lesser extent, but in essentially the same way, by creatures," as Simon Oliver puts it. Paradoxically, this doesn't bring God closer but pushes him further away. "God comes to be understood in anthropomorphic terms as rather like an infinitely large person, a cause alongside other causes in the universe, or an object amongst other objects in the field of our attention." Contrast this with the ideas of Thomas Aquinas, who argued that God and His creatures are fundamentally different. You might think that God would become unapproachable when seen in this way—as a being quite different from the father God of the Bible—but the opposite is actually the case. If God is essentially like us, though far greater, he becomes unattainable. If His infinite being is markedly different from our finite being, He can save us through His free gift of grace. By allowing us to participate in his life, He brings us into union with Him.

Radical Orthodoxy is sometimes criticized for being forbiddingly intellectual, and it is true that John Milbank's writings make huge demands on the reader. However, it is also true that ideas have consequences. The way we think about God really matters. If we believe that God created the universe and then stepped aside, if we believe that independent reason can explain the world without any reference to God, that is bound to affect the way we live our lives. What Radical Orthodoxy offers, by contrast, is a profound analysis of the modern world and how we got here, enabling us to fight back against the siren voices of secularism.

However, Radical Orthodoxy is not simply an ideas-based movement, because of the emphasis it places on participation. As John Milbank, Graham Ward, and Catherine Pickstock argue in their introduction to *Radical Orthodoxy*, "the central theological frame-

## Radical Orthodoxy

work of radical orthodoxy is 'participation' as developed by Plato and reworked by Christianity, because any alternative configuration perforce reserves a territory independent of God." We are constantly tempted to create "a zone apart from God" but doing so would be the most self-destructive action we could possibly take. It is only by participating in the life of God that we can become truly free. In other words, what RO says makes a difference in what we do. Its focus on participation also helps us to see the significance of the radically Christian groups we have met in this book. They are radical insofar as they participate in the life and work of God, in His very being. It is not their withdrawing from the world that matters. It's not even being counter-cultural. It's letting go of self-will so that they can participate in the life-giving, life-enhancing presence of God in the world.

Radical Orthodoxy is a positive, hope-filled movement. It believes that human beings have an essential nobility that is often best expressed in what we do and what we make. Our creativity participates in the creativity of God. Of course, RO thinkers aren't the first to have pointed this out. Many years ago, during a late-night walk around Magdalen College deer park in Oxford, J.R.R. Tolkien convinced C.S. Lewis of the importance of such a participation in God's creativity and so helped him cross the line from unbelief to Christianity. After their walk, Tolkien turned his thoughts into a poem, which contains these inspiring lines:

> The heart of man is not compound of lies,
> but draws some wisdom from the only Wise,
> and still recalls him. Though now long estranged,
> man is not wholly lost nor wholly changed.
> Dis-graced he may be, yet is not dethroned,
> and keeps the rags of lordship once he owned,
> his world-dominion by creative act:
> not his to worship the great Artefact,
> man, sub-creator, the refracted light
> through whom is splintered from a single White
> to many hues, and endlessly combined
> in living shapes that move from mind to mind.

Though all the crannies of the world we filled
with elves and goblins, though we dared to build
gods and their houses out of dark and light,
and sow the seed of dragons, 'twas our right
(used or misused). The right has not decayed.
We make still by the law in which we're made.

**There are no ordinary people**
So how do we participate in the life of God? There are many ways in which we can do so: through the service of the poor; through acts of creativity; and also, importantly, through worship. Radical Orthodoxy places a great deal of emphasis on the liturgy, on the importance of praise. As Johannes Hoff, another RO thinker, explains: "Liturgy discloses what deserves our attention and esteem, and helps us to distinguish between essential and ephemeral occurrences and phenomena." Praise precedes reason. What we see, then, is a way in which we can unite the insights of such apparently disparate groups as the Transalpine Redemptorists and the Bruderhof, the Franciscan Sisters of the Renewal and the Catholic Worker Movement. What unites them all is a desire to participate in the life and work of God, a participation which must necessarily lead to acts of public worship (which, after all, is what liturgy means) and acts of charity. Differences of theology and emphasis there certainly are but, Radical Orthodoxy might suggest, there is also enough shared ground to build a lived critique of godless, secular modernity. This certainly doesn't mean we should ignore doctrinal or liturgical differences, but it does mean we need not be swamped by them.

Radical Orthodoxy also suggests how we can move forward in our secular age with a renewed understanding of freedom. Many people now think of freedom as self-empowerment. We choose who we want to be. This sense of negative freedom (freedom *from* rather than freedom *for*) is not the traditional Christian understanding of freedom. As Johannes Hoff explains it, "we are not condemned to determine ourselves as this or that; rather we are called to become what we are," namely gods and goddesses.

Now that's a shocking idea to most people today, but for most of Christian history, deification (or *theosis* in Greek) was an absolutely standard belief. As the *Catechism of the Catholic Church* puts it, quoting the Second Letter of Peter and St Athanasius, "[t]he Word became flesh to make us *'partakers of the divine nature'* […] 'For the Son of God became man so that we might become God.'" Johannes Hoff, writing about the great fifteenth-century cardinal Nicholas of Cusa, puts it like this: "We are oriented to the deification (*theosis*) of our embodied existence from the outset." We become truly free when we allow God to make us who we were always meant to be, who we already potentially are. One modern thinker who understood this well is C.S. Lewis. In "The Weight of Glory," a talk he gave during World War II, he said:

> It is a serious thing to live in a society of possible gods and goddesses, to remember that the dullest and most uninteresting person you talk to may one day be a creature which, if you saw it now, you would be strongly tempted to worship, or else a horror and a corruption such as you now meet, if at all, only in a nightmare. All day long we are, in some degree, helping each other to one or other of these destinations. It is in the light of these overwhelming possibilities, it is with the awe and the circumspection proper to them, that we should conduct all our dealings with one another, all friendships, all loves, all play, all politics. There are no *ordinary* people. You have never talked to a mere mortal. Nations, cultures, arts, civilization—these are mortal, and their life is to ours as the life of a gnat. But it is immortals whom we joke with, work with, marry, snub, and exploit—immortal horrors or everlasting splendours.

If everyone we meet is a possible god or goddess, it must fundamentally affect the way we respond to them. The life we live can no longer be the same. And our aspirations can no longer be the same either. As C.S. Lewis points out in that same talk:

> If we consider the unblushing promises of reward and the staggering nature of the rewards promised in the Gospels, it would seem that Our Lord finds our desires, not too strong, but too weak. We are half-hearted creatures, fooling about with drink and sex and ambition when infinite joy is offered us, like an igno-

rant child who wants to go on making mud pies in a slum because he cannot imagine what is meant by the offer of a holiday at the sea. We are far too easily pleased.

In response to Rod Dreher's rhetoric of crisis in *The Benedict Option*, Radical Orthodoxy offers a rhetoric of radical hope, a picture of possibilities that are beyond human imagining. We can participate in the life of God Himself, we are called to become gods and goddesses in union with Him, we do not need to live as if everything is lost.

**Dionysius the Areopagite**

It is no surprise, then, to learn that Radical Orthodoxy looks to the work of Dionysius the Areopagite (or Pseudo-Dionysius as he is sometimes called) for inspiration. According to Alison Milbank, Dionysius defines the heart of Radical Orthodoxy's mystical practice: "an understanding of our calling as Christians to share in the life of God himself through participation (*methexis*) and deification (*theosis*)." But there's more to Dionysius than a theology of participation and deification, Simon Oliver reminds us. He also wrote about "a hierarchy of harmonious differences of natures, talents, characters, wills, desires and so on." What had been bugging me ever since my visit to the Catholic Worker Movement (and even before that, because the Bruderhof hold similar beliefs) was a concern about the flattening tendencies of some radically Christian groups, especially those who have developed deep suspicions of the institutional Church. This suspicion would have made little sense to Nicholas of Cusa who, as Simon Oliver explains, believed that, "within the hierarchical social or ecclesial body, an individual found a role, place and identity and, as such, was set free to be a *particular person* within a social or ecclesial whole. One's personal identity was understood more as a gift than a matter of the invention of the individual will." Between theologians like Dionysius the Areopagite and Nicholas of Cusa, on the one hand, and many people in the twenty-first century, on the other, there is an apparently unbridgeable gulf: "We ... tend to think of hierarchy as necessarily authoritarian and the embodiment of inequality. In the end, for a thinker such as Cusa there was only one fundamental, irreducible difference within the hierarchy, namely that between God and creation."

Many modern political and ethical debates start with the assumption that difference is problematic, but this assumption is itself the problem, Simon Oliver suggests:

> In the modern period, difference—the difference between natures, cultures, viewpoints, desires, interests, skills, genders, wills and so on—came to be understood as harboring the seeds not of mutually enhancing and harmonious unity, but of conflict. Difference could be regarded as the engine of friction, the source of envy, resentment and disagreement. This led to what is sometimes referred to as the "flattening" tendency of modernity, namely the desire to eradicate difference in favor of homogeneity and uniformity. The metaphor of "flattening" is a deliberate contrast with the hierarchical and differentiated understanding of the Church, society and cosmos which dominated ancient thought and the mediaeval consensus.

Radically Orthodox thinkers ask what would happen if we challenged this basic assumption of the modern world. What would happen if we returned to traditional Christian understandings of peaceable difference, as seen primarily in the Holy Trinity itself? One answer is that we would end up with a very different form of politics, grounded in a very different form of economics. Here's Alison Milbank again:

> RO denies the nihilism in competitive modes of economic theory, arguing for mutuality, reciprocity and virtue in markets and economic practice. Its politics varies between adherents but is always radical. It crosses political divides, standing for the importance of the family, local community and subsidiarity and tradition in ways that would be thought conservative, even valuing virtuous hierarchy, while severely and radically critiquing capitalism.

There is currently a surge of interest in so-called post-liberal politics, led by thinkers such as Adrian Pabst and John Milbank in the UK and Adrian Vermeule, Patrick Deneen, Gladden Pappin, Chad

Pecknold, and Sohrab Ahmari in the USA. Post-liberalism often draws on the deep well of Catholic Social Teaching, which continues to influence thinkers and politicians from a wide range of backgrounds. In the UK, for example, Lord Glasman, a Jewish member of the House of Lords, has written extensively about his indebtedness to CST, while Labour politicians such as Jon Cruddas and Conservatives such as Danny Kruger and Miriam Cates have all been influenced by what Catholic Social Teaching has to say about the common good. What underlies much of the work of this disparate group is a belief in the possibility of peaceable difference and, therefore, in communitarian responses to our current social, economic, and political woes. There is a strong sense that it is possible to rebuild community without having to withdraw from a world dominated by secular liberalism.

We have moved beyond the often narrow confines of academic theology here, but that shouldn't surprise anyone who has an interest in Radical Orthodoxy. If the subject matter of theology is God and all things in relation to God, then it would be a concern if it didn't have something to say about politics, economics, and the law (as well as something to say about creativity, the liturgy, and our final destination). We have also, perhaps, come to a point where we can look afresh at the challenge thrown down by Rod Dreher in *The Benedict Option*. If theology is the queen of the sciences, if it has something to say about everything, then maybe we don't need to retreat to be counter-cultural. Maybe we can be radically Christian precisely where we are. Having traveled across the UK in search of radical Christianity, I realized that it was time to return to my own parish. I needed to investigate whether radical Christianity had been on my doorstep all along. But before I went back home at last, there was just one more detour I needed to make.

# 12

# Back to the Parish

THE FINAL LEG of my journey took place, paradoxically, during the first Covid lockdown when no one could travel anywhere. As many churches went into a survival mode, the parish church where one of our relatives worshiped, St Elizabeth of Portugal in Richmond, south London, looked to expand, appointing a dynamic Director of Youth Ministry and starting an online youth group. Sensing an opportunity at a time when it was impossible to meet in person, one of my daughters asked if she could join. When lockdown ended and the youth group started to meet in person, we suddenly had a decision to make: did we return to the status quo or did we bite the bullet and drive our daughter to Richmond every Monday evening so she could be part of this lively, faith-filled group? A two-and-a-half-hour round trip might not be a big deal in the USA but to travel-shy Brits, it seemed a big ask. However, the more we thought about it, the simpler the decision became. There was nothing like it near us, so it would have been ridiculous not to put ourselves out. A youth group which presents the fullness of the faith in a way that teenagers enjoy is a treasure indeed.

As time went on, the commitment expanded. The youth group started having weekend socials. Then they organized a retreat. Eventually, they joined forces with theASCENT, a three-year post-Confirmation program, which meant more retreats and weekly meetings. While other parishes were desperately trying to hang on to their youngsters while also attempting to encourage the parishioners who never came back after lockdown, St Elizabeth's was going full steam ahead with its program of evangelization, youth work, and parish renewal.

Driving to Richmond soon became part of our weekly ritual. We worked our way through various audiobooks and then, realizing that we were now in this for the long haul, launched into *The Lord of the Rings*. Those car journeys now took on a new significance as we left the shire with Frodo and Sam, battled our way through to Rivendell, and then set off on the long journey to Mordor. We weren't just going to and from youth group, we were taking part in an epic adventure. Is that a hyperbole? Maybe. But there is also some truth in it. What this small parish in south London was doing was inspiring. Rather than accept the secularizing drift of modernity, rather than give all his time to managing the parish's decline, Fr Stephen Langridge, the parish priest, had decided to fight back, to preach the Gospel with confidence and to build up a team that could help him to reach beyond the walls of the church while also building the faith of his parishioners. Slowly, inevitably perhaps, I was drawn into this program of renewal too.

Can radical Christianity of the kind I had seen during my travels flourish in a parish setting? Can parishes be radically counter-cultural? Should we be seeking the renewal of the Church through the renewal of the parish? I wasn't sure but I knew I had to investigate further, not least because it was also becoming increasingly clear that the parish itself is under threat from various directions.

Shortly after St Elizabeth of Portugal launched its youth group, a group of Anglicans, including Alison Milbank, my doctoral supervisor, launched Save the Parish, a campaigning organization opposed to what they called a "power grab, which would deny local churches and communities the power and right to contest plans to close their churches, make their priests redundant, or throw their priests out of their homes." Having converted to Catholicism from Anglicanism many years ago, I was surprised to discover that the Church of England had now embraced a model of "renewal" that favored gathered communities which might or might not meet on Sundays and might or might not be run by priests. I found it hard to find fault with Danny Kruger's analysis of the Church of England's current malaise:

> The Church of England's plans to allow bishops to merge or abolish local parishes without the consent of parishioners is a bad trend, an echo of all the failed centralizations of the last 50 years

that make British public services so bureaucratic and out of touch. The new spirit of the age, which the Church needs to catch up with, is localism, trust, and "power to the people." The best approach is not to centralize but localize—empower the front-line, trust the vicars and PCCs [Parochial Church Councils], maintain the presence of the Church of England in the places where people live.

However, it wasn't just the Church of England that was struggling with its parish model. The Catholic Church too has been increasingly closing or merging parishes, with many dioceses now managing an apparently inevitable decline. With hard questions being asked about the future of the parish by everyone from bishops worried about priestly vocations to traditionalists worried about the pope's attitude towards the Traditional Latin Mass, the future can seem desperately uncertain.

**Divine Renovation**
It was against this backdrop that I spoke to Georgia Clarke, project manager for parish renewal in the Archdiocese of Southwark and Director of Youth Ministry at St Elizabeth of Portugal. What is the future of the parish? I wondered. Is parish renewal possible? What has happened at St Elizabeth of Portugal and can that model be replicated elsewhere? Georgia answered those questions by telling me about Divine Renovation, an organization founded by Fr James Mallon in Canada, which argues that there are three keys to parish renewal: the power of the Holy Spirit, the primacy of evangelization, and the best of leadership. With these three keys, Divine Renovation accompanies "priests and lay leaders who desire to see their parish come alive by providing them with the tools and coaching they need to lead their parish from maintenance to mission," the website explains.

Fundamental to the Divine Renovation approach is the notion that "in order to thrive, a parish must fully embrace its missionary identity. Instead of managing decline and maintaining the methods and practices that were best suited for a time in the Church's life that has since passed, parishes must live a culture of mission and evangelization." Taking these ideas seriously was clearly what led Fr

Stephen Langridge to employ a Director of Youth Ministry and preach incessantly about evangelization during the Covid crisis when many parishes were working out how to stay in contact with their parishioners and pay the bills.

Divine Renovation's focus on leadership, Georgia told me, is revolutionary for many parishes but it's not revolutionary at all in the world. As the Divine Renovation website puts it, "if it's important for a company that sells sneakers to have the best of leadership, how much more important is it for priests—who shepherd people to God and deal with questions of the eternal?" "But isn't this just managerialism creeping into the Church?" I asked, thinking about some of the problems Save the Parish was encountering in the Church of England. "No," Georgia replied, because ministry comes from the priest's ordination. Parishes which embrace the Divine Renovation approach are not turning their priests into managers, but are trying to unlock the potential for leadership that is already there, not just in the priest but in parishioners too. That is why St Elizabeth of Portugal and other parishes now have senior leadership teams.

Since this still sounded a lot like managerialism, I asked what the difference was between a parish council and a senior leadership team. "Parish councils are usually very operational," Georgia replied. They focus on what needs to be done next, but with a senior leadership team in place, the priest is able to delegate some of his own leadership, which enables him to develop more of a vision for the parish and also frees him to fulfill his priestly role. That made sense. Too many priests are too weighed down by worries about the church fabric, paying the electricity bills, and keeping the finance committee happy to be able to do what they were ordained to do. That is why Divine Renovation and similar organizations emphasize the importance of the art of preaching and the art of giving. The importance of good preaching may be obvious, but the art of giving makes Brits feel distinctly uncomfortable. Nonetheless, Georgia insisted on its importance, giving me some shocking statistics about the average weekly donation in British parishes. Even for each family to give £1 more each week would make a big difference, though she also suggested that asking parishioners to give to a particular ministry, such as youth work, tends to make a big difference in the work of the parish. With the priest freed from financial concerns, he can actually start to lead his parish from maintenance to mission, though only in the power of the Holy Spirit. Divine Renovation is quite clear that "it is only through the power of the Holy Spirit that the work of mission, evangelization, and parish renewal bears fruit."

"And what about youth work?" I asked. "What have you been trying to achieve at St Elizabeth's?"

When she started at St Elizabeth's, Georgia was quite clear that she didn't want to run a discrete Confirmation program. "Why run a twelve-step program to losing teenagers forever?" she asked rhetorically, adding, "you're not the dentist." Instead she wanted to create a program that had a relationship with Christ as its starting point. Without that relationship, nothing else would work. With it, confirmations would naturally occur. And so it has proved. Lots of teenagers (and adults) are confirmed at St Elizabeth's but they don't then disappear. Because they are valued within the parish, because there are regular opportunities for them to meet, socialize, and pray together, because they are given opportunities to go to confession and go on retreat, because there is a weekly teen Mass, they are an integral part of the community.

The question of what happens after Confirmation isn't, therefore, so pressing a problem at St Elizabeth's as it might be elsewhere. With the teenagers already embedded in the life of the parish, they are less likely to drift away from the faith. Nonetheless, there is still work to be done, which is why St Elizabeth's has teamed up with theASCENT. Having accepted the faith for themselves, the teenagers are now ready to grow in discipleship, the longer-term aim being that they become leaders within the Church, having the faith, confidence, and tools they need to be able to bring others to Christ.

Peer-to-peer ministry lies at the heart of theASCENT, the young people socializing with and supporting each other, but there is also a recognition that teenagers value one-to-one time with adult mentors too, especially when these adults are still young enough to understand their concerns and speak their language. One of the most impressive aspects of the work Georgia has done in the parish is to create a team of leaders around her. Having leaders who are in their twenties and on fire with their faith clearly makes a huge difference to teenagers. Neither the parish priest nor parents are sidelined in this process—far from it—but the parish has been flexible enough to respond to the needs of the young people to whom it ministers during a time of national decline.

**We don't need strobe lighting and smoke machines at Mass**
Having chatted to Georgia, I drove my daughter to a residential weekend for theASCENT at the Sion Catholic Community for Evangelism in the UK and then joined them again for their closing Mass, which the Bishop of Arundel and Brighton celebrated. As this was a national gathering of many young people, Mass was held in a large marquee with people spilling out into the garden as there wasn't enough room inside. To be honest, the style of worship at that Mass wasn't quite my cup of tea. There was lots of praise music and arms being raised in the air. I would have preferred the silences of the traditional Latin Mass, but theASCENT weekend wasn't aimed toward people like me. The teenagers from Richmond were certainly reverent, having experienced the dignity and solemnity of worship in their home parish, but here in the marquee they also sang worship songs with gusto.

As the teenagers left theASCENT weekend with a faithful fire in their belly, I couldn't help but compare the Mass with ones I had attended at St Elizabeth's. One of the strengths of the parish is the way it combines evangelistic outreach and a vibrant youth ministry with sound teaching and devotion at Mass. The music sung by the professional choir at the Sunday morning Masses is about as far from happy-clappy as you can get, the full riches of Catholic devotional music drawing hearts to Christ, just as the homilies speak to the mind, and the reverence of the liturgy reminds us of what is still possible in a parish setting. The music on offer at the evening youth Masses is quite different but even here there is room for silence and reverence. "We don't need strobe lighting and smoke machines at Mass," Georgia Clarke told me. The way to bring young people into the Church in the first place, or into a deeper relationship with Christ, is not to dumb down theology or ape celebrity culture, but

## Back to the Parish

to draw on the full riches of the Faith and to present it to them in ways they can understand and in contexts where they know themselves to be truly valued members of the body of Christ. It seemed both radical and achievable.

Back to the parish: is that the battle cry I should now be shouting? I wondered as I headed back home. I thought about all the places I had been: the Bruderhof communities with their high-tech factories and low-tech homes; the Franciscans of the Renewal with their joyful service of the poor; the Manquehue Apostolic Movement with its renewal of Benedictine monasticism in a lay setting; Opus Dei with its focus on the universal call to holiness; the Catholic Worker Movement with its radical activism; the Transalpine Redemptorists with their devotion to the traditional liturgy; my fellow home-educators with their determination to be the primary educators of their children; L'Arche with its radical inclusion of people with and without learning disabilities; Margaret and Barry Mizen with their inspiring message of forgiveness, peace, and hope; Radical Orthodoxy with its profound analysis of the modern world, how we got here, and what we can do next. I thought about all the places I had been and all the people I had met, and gave thanks for each of them. I had found radical Christians all round the country and now, at last, I had realized that it was possible to be radically Christian precisely where I was as well.

Living in a fallen world, we find it hard to see the path ahead of us. We walk with faltering steps, taking wrong turnings as often as right ones. The lamp of faith is strong but sometimes we try to quench it in frustration, irritation, or anger. Unsure where to go, we too often ignore our fellow travelers and blunder on alone. But sometimes the gloom that surrounds us lifts for a moment and we realize that we are not alone. We are surrounded not just by others like us who are fallible and apt to get lost, but also by a cloud of witnesses who have gone before us. Above all, we sometimes glimpse Our Lord himself, closer to us than we had ever dared hope, walking with us every step of the way. Having traveled in radical Christianity, I can offer no easy answers, no pat suggestions, that can be applied like a coat of paint to any situation, but I can perhaps echo that great English saint, John Henry Newman, who also struggled to find his way at times but who never entirely lost sight of the Kindly Light which eventually led him home:

> Lead, Kindly Light, amid the encircling gloom
> Lead Thou me on!
> The night is dark, and I am far from home—
> Lead Thou me on!
> Keep Thou my feet; I do not ask to see
> The distant scene—one step enough for me.

Printed in Great Britain
by Amazon